Mal Review

Vol. 5 No. 2 Autumn 2014

Black-lava Malpaís/badlands in western New Mexico

"The Badlands are everywhere"

Malpaís Review
po box 339
Placitas, NM 87043

The Meaning of *Malpaís*

The Spanish word "malpaís" (badlands) is a term that can have wide and narrow meaning. Badlands can be inside and outside, artistic, psychological, geographical, political and historical. The literal black-lava badlands in New Mexico are most prominent in the western part of the state where the Malpaís National Monument is located. The famous badlands of South Dakota (which are not volcanic), and others, take different forms but have common meaning.

There are many applications of the word "malpaís." Politically, the nation has gone through a long period of badlands in the last 25 years or so, which has greatly eroded what little remains of American democracy. Artists go through periodic "badlands" of blank page or blank canvas, though these are not permanent. But whatever the literal or metaphorical nature of the term, the badlands are everywhere.

The texts in this publication, we hope, will help to discover personal and collective badlands, so they can be dealt with and maybe offer some guidance or serve as some sort of sustenance in crossing the badlands, wherever they are located and whatever meaning they have for our readers.

Malpaís **Review** is available thru Amazon.com and these bookstores: Treasure House Books (Old Town) Albuquerque, NM; Range Cafe Store, Bernalillo, NM; Arte de Placitas Gallery, Placitas, NM; Op Cit Bookstore (500 Montezuma) Santa Fe, NM; Moby Dickens Bookstore (124A Bent St) Taos, NM; Anthology Books (3941 SE Hawthorne Blvd) Portland, OR; and Beyond Baroque, Los Angeles, CA.

Subscriptions:
> $42 for one year (4 issues) postage paid
> $55 to institutions for one year (" ") " "

Single copies by mail:
> $12 + $3.50 shipping and handling
>   Make checks payable to Gary Brower, and mail to
>   *Malpaís* Review, po box 339, Placitas, NM 87043

For Contributor Biographies, Submission Guidelines, and Photo, Art and Poem Credits, please see last pages of this issue.

ISSN 2153-4918   Malpaísreview.com

Malpaís Review
Vol. 5 No. 2 Autumn 2014

Editorial Staff:

    Editor: Gary L. Brower

    Guest Editor and Associate Editor: Dale Harris

    Pacific Northwest Editor: Marilyn Stablein

    Southern California Correspondent: Suzanne Lummis

    Staff Photographer: J. M. Gay, Jr

    Graphic Designer and Assistant Editor: Esther Feske

    Webmaster: J. M. Gay, Jr

Advisory Board:

    Renny Golden

    E. A. "Tony" Mares

    Simon Ortiz

    Charles Potts

    Margaret Randall

Malpaís Review name and slogan: Todd Moore

The lively and colorful images on the covers are from the "Heart Suit" by Denise Weaver Ross– front: "Six Phases of the Eclipse of the Heart," back: "The Queen of Heart Transplants." In this series, Denise recreates the entire deck of cards as 26-by-40-inch mixed-media works on paper. The Heart Suit combines her personal story with Egyptian and Tarot images. Clubs become the Tree Suit showing myth and story from different cultures. The Diamond suit becomes a Star Suit with a focus on celestial bodies and constellations. Finally, Spades become a Bone Suit, using fossil prehistory with Day of the Dead imagery.

Karen Koshgarian of Portland, Oregon, recently drove Route 66 from Chicago to Santa Monica. From 10,000+ photographs, she created a book called *Drive-by Shooting on Old Route 66 - A Camera's Point-of-View.* Every photograph was literally taken either from the car, or by the car. A poetic tome, images are meant to be savored. We are pleased to present seven of these photographs.

> The Editor is interested in poems about classical music or composers for a future issue. Send poems to poetry@ MalpaísReview.com and mark the submissions as "classical."

Contents

6

EDITOR'S NOTE: *MR* V5#2

"The perfect is the enemy of the good." –Ansel Adams

With this issue of *MR*, we finish the Feminist anthology begun in the Summer issue. We had no idea that it would end up being so large, but when it did, there was no other choice but to divide it in two. Our preference was to have it all in one issue but, given the other features and poems accepted in each issue, that was not possible. Because Part II is even bigger than Part I, we had to change original plans for this Fall issue.

In addition, we have a deceased featured poet in this issue for the first time, Keith Wilson, one of the best New Mexico poets ever. And he's one of the best poets to write poetry about the Korean War, in which he served.

We have two other features that are different and unique: a consideration of the ghazal poetic form (by poet Robin MacGowan), and one of its famous practitioners from another century, Saeb (with poems in translation); and poems by Cuban poet Nancy Morejón, one of Cuba's best and most famous poets today, who sent us poems directly for publication in *MR*. Morejón, who is Afro-Cuban, is a specialist on the poetry of Cuba's famous National Poet Nicolás Guillén (1902-1989), one of the prominent leaders of the Afro-Antillean poetry movement in the 1930s. He was also a mentor to Morejón early in her career and she has published two books on Guillén's work since his demise.

What most readers will likely not know, because it's rarely linked together in literary histories, is that in the 1920s and 1930s, there was a global movement of African and Afro-cultural poets, and artists of all genres, in the western hemisphere and in Africa, with reverberating influences in Europe. (Also, the beginnings of seminal liberation awakenings in colonial empires around the world). This African influence took two forms: as the "Great War" (WWI) loosened dominance in "the colonies," things began to foment. Local native leaders had been educated and began to think of the future without outside control. When colonial Native Troops saw that they had to be called upon to help their colonizers, saw the defeat of their "masters" at the hands of other militaries from time to time, it became clear that these colonial powers were not invincible. Some native leaders in European colonies also remembered the defeat of

Russia by the Japanese in the Russo-Japanese War (1905), the first time a European power lost to a non-European nation, a shock to the established world order of the time.

In Europe especially, the arrival of the avant-garde artistic movements (Dada, Surrealism, etc.) between the world wars was in opposition to the perversion of the Western Rationalist Tradition; the disaster of the first mechanized war (WWI, 1914-18), with 17 million dead, resulted in an alienation from western Rationalist thought by artists and a turn to non-Rationalist societies, cultures and realities. In other words, artists responded to the military carnage by trying to find alternate "realities" to re-balance their cultures, away from what was supposed be logical (Reason, Science) but which had resulted in the illogic of mass killing (linked to nationalism, military egos, entangling alliances, and the repression of populations by old Empires). Technology was good for the advancement of Science but bad for people when applied to war! If Reason became unreasonable, then it was time to investigate ideas in which that tradition was not dominant.

The places where European artists looked was non-European cultures because they were historically separate from the Western Rationalist Tradition in their base. Most traditional tribal cultures have religious/spiritual currents within a mythic system of belief and circular/mythic rather than linear/chronometric time. The alienation also took the form of interest in non-rational "realities" such as dreams and the subconscious elaborated by Sigmund Freud and others, and similar tendencies–child and child-like art, pathological art, Outsider Art, Naive Art, etc. If the predominantly logical lobe of the human brain had failed to prevent a horrific global war, then artists turned to the more intuitional lobe of the brain for artistic impetus to carry them away from disaster and chaos. Perhaps they should have remembered the title of one of Goya's most famous *Caprichos* series of etchings about war: "The Dreams of Reason produce monsters" (1808).

So there was a re-evaluation of so-called "primitive cultures" and their cultural artifacts, helped along at the time by numerous museum exhibits of cultural objects originally brought to Europe to show the nature of the subjugated peoples in their colonies. Many of the European avant-garde artists, especially Picasso, Matisse, Modigliani, Brancusi, among others, absorbed the art of Africa and other so-called "Primitivist" societies, which could be seen in their works. (And anticipated by Gauguin in Tahiti.) From Europe, the tendency jumped to the U.S. and significantly to visual and literary artists in the Harlem Renaissance. Said one commentator: "what appears in European art as abstraction is in Primitive art nature rendered directly." (Robert Goldwater, *Primitivism in Modern Art*, New York, Vintage, 1967, p. 36). The term "primitive," it should be noted, has been very controversial over the years, often seen as a negative term, though later re-evaluated. But when the influenced artists used the term, it was very positive.

In literature as well as in the visual arts and politics, the colonized native cultures of the Caribbean and Africa began to boil with the rise of interest in local realities and traditions that were suppressed or ignored by the colonial powers. So, while "Primitive art" was being newly appreciated by European and American artists, developments began within the areas of "native cultures" themselves, bringing up their own histories and non-Western traditions. Within this context, there developed, in addition to the Harlem Renaissance (1918-1937)* in the U.S., the movement of *Poesie de la Negritude* in the French Caribbean, Francophone Africa; *Poesía Afro-Antillana* in the Spanish-speaking Caribbean and various anglophone poets in the English-speaking Caribbean, not to mention the Afro-Brazilian poets and a few Afro-Dutch poets from the Dutch West Indies, as well as Afro-Peruvian, Afro-Colombian, Afro-Venezuelan, and Afro-Ecuadorean writers. This is the larger macro-focus for the appearance of a poet such as Nicolás Guillén in Cuba, and eventually for a poet such as Nancy Morejón today.

Richard L. Jackson, in his study, *The Black Image in Latin American Literature* (Albuquerque, University of New Mexico Press, 1976), says that Nicolás Guillén, "...for many years has preached the synthesis or the realization of the universal man in an antiracist society where brotherhood rather than narrow racialism is sought." (p. 125). Guillén, in other words, was an early fighter against racism, dating from the 1930s at least, not only in Cuba but in a wider context. Jackson cites two poems as examples: "Ode to a black Cuban boxer" and "New Woman" (which could be compared with Morejón's "Black Woman," one of her most powerful poems against slavery-see my introduction to Morejón in this issue). In one of Guillén's most interesting books, *Songoro Cosongo* (1931), he includes one of his most famous poems, "Sensemayá," based on a ritual of *Lucumí* or *Santería* (the Cuban equivalent of Haitian *voudun* or Brazilian *Candomblé*), African-origin religious practices, in this case to sacrifice a snake to a god, perhaps *Babalú Aye*. The *Mayombero* is the one who carries out the ritual. Here's a segment from the poem (my translation):

> Song to kill a snake by
> Mayombe Bombe Mayombé
> The snake has eyes of glass
> The snake comes and wraps around a stick (....)

> With his eyes of glass
> The snake travel without legs
> The snake hides in the grass
> traveling without legs
> Mayombe Bombe Mayombé (....)

> Kill it Now!

The structure of this poem based on ritual is very similar to the traditional structure of "primitive song" (See C. M. Bowra's *Primitive Song* (New York, World, 1962)), with more repetition than variation and basic descriptions of the snake which seem obvious but are typical of these texts. Guillén said he was a "Cuban Yoruba" and always wrote from an Afro-Cuban perspective, but he also, as noted by Jackson, was someone whose "humanist values make him a universal man free in his color but in close solidarity with his brothers of all colors, particularly the oppressed." In many ways, Nancy Morejón follows in Guillén's footsteps in these beliefs. Other important Afro-Antillean poets include the Puerto Rican Luís Palés Matos (1898-1959), a major Caribbean poet, Cuban Emilio Ballagas (1908-1954), and Dominican Manual del Cabral (1907-1999), and in later times, the Afro-Ecuadorean poet/novelist/diplomat Adalberto Ortiz (1914-2003), who was not in the Afro-Antillean tendency, given that he was from an Andean country.

In addition to the Afro-Caribbean Spanish-speaking poets, there was also the very important *Poesie de la Negritude* equivalent for francophone writers (1920s-1930s), which produced some major poets. The Harlem Renaissance artists, introduced to French writers by the Nardal sisters, greatly influenced the *Negritude* (Blackness) writers who formed the movement in France in the 1930s. Some Haitian writers were likewise influential. Specifically, there were three poets who founded the movement, at first important as writers and (later) as politicians: Martinican Aimé Césaire (1913-2008); French Guyanese Leon Damas (1912-1978); and Senegalese Leopold Sedar Senghor (1906-2006). They began the movement while studying at universities in Paris and founded a publication titled *L'Etudiant Noir* (The Black Student), a seminal publication in the galvanizing of Afro-Francophone leaders. Later, all of these poets held political offices, beginning as Members of Parliament (Césaire was also Mayor of the capital of Martinique, Fort-de-France). Also, Césaire and Senghor founded socialist parties in their own nations. Senghor became the first President of an independent Senegal and served in that office for 20 years (1960-1980). Another significant Senegalese poet and novelist was Birago Diop (1906-1989). These men changed not only the self-image of black French citizens but of francophone literature: they took the term *negre*, often used negatively, and converted it into a positive by inventing *Negritude* as an umbrella term, associated with good writers and leaders. Since most of these men were of the political Left, their movement clearly was a rejection of French colonialism. A synthesis of the *Negritude* movement was a famous anthology published in 1948, edited by Senghor, titled *Anthologie de la nouvelle poesie negre et malagache* (Anthology of New Black and Malagasy Poetry), with an introduction by Jean Paul Sartre, who defended the movement.

And, as far as anglophone poets and writers in the Caribbean are concerned, we need only remember that more recently St. Lucian poet Derek Walcott won the Nobel Prize for Literature (1992), and the popularity of the works of East Indian/Caribbean prose writer V. S. Naipaul.

All of these poets are part of the context for the role and importance of Cuban poet Nicolás Guillén and by extension also for Nancy Morejón. It is a wider and deeper cultural background than most people probably know and, hopefully, this discussion of it will put her poetry into a larger perspective. But we also have to remember that she is not just a black poet, not just a Cuban poet, not just a female poet, and not just a socially committed poet, but all four. And, of course, most important is that fact that she is an excellent poet.

12

On November 14, one of the most well known poets in the U.S., Naomi Shehab Nye (b. 1952, St. Louis) visited Albuquerque and spoke at the KiMo Theater to a full house, the event sponsored by the New Mexico Humanities Council. For an hour and a half, Nye spoke and read poems, telling how the creative process works for her, talking about her family and Palestinian-American background (through her journalist father), about the violence in Palestine, and urging peace. She also talked about experiences with children, especially as she has published books for them. Nye, who now lives in San Antonio, Texas, is extremely articulate and a good reader of her work. She was also interviewed on stage by journalist Megan Kamerick and answered questions from the audience. This is not the first time Nye has been in New Mexico, and in fact she is a fan of the state and likes visiting: in one poem about the Albuquerque airport titled "Gate A-4" she recounts a personal experience she had with a Palestinian woman passing through whose plane was delayed. An announcement over the airport loudspeaker asked for anyone who speaks Arabic to help, and Nye responded. The woman was upset because she only spoke Arabic and didn't understand what was happening. Nye was able to help since she speaks Arabic. She calmed the woman and defused the situation to the point where everyone involved was laughing and eating cookies. I think this sums up Shehab Nye's nature: she is a peacemaker. But it also symbolizes how she helps the Palestinian people when possible and on whatever level she can. Her husband, Michael Nye is a photographer and documentary film maker.

We lost two major U.S. poets recently, both a great loss because of the quality of their work and their commitment to people and to change. Many years ago, I heard Galway Kinnell (1927-2014) read his work, in Oregon I think, though I can't remember whether it was in Portland or Eugene. He was an impressive, big guy, almost like a football lineman for a poetry team, and then when he read, he was even bigger, though in another way. He started with his most famous poem, "The Avenue bearing the initial of Christ into the New World," a 14-part work, though he didn't read it all (it hadn't all been written then). Then he read two of his other most famous poems, from *Body Rags*, "The Bear" and "The Porcupine." He was, I think, one of this nation's best poets of recent years, and a powerful reader.

He never affiliated or was associated with any grouping of poets and was, rather, the sort of person who is always independent. The *New York Times* obit (10/30/14, p. 27) noted that he "came of age among a generation of poets who were trying to get past the modernism of T. S. Eliot and Ezra Pound and write verses that, as he said, could be understood without a graduate degree." Kinnell won the Pulitzer Prize in 1963 for his "Selected Poems" and a share of the National Book Award. He said, "I think if you are ever going to find any kind of truth in poetry it has to be based on all of experience rather than on a narrow segment of cheerful events." Born in Providence, RI (the only poet from that state I've ever met I think), he went to a prep school in his youth and, an odd coincidence, his roommate was poet W. S. Merwin. Some of his favorite poets were Yeats, Rilke, Villon. He graduated from Princeton, after Navy service in WWII and a Fulbright to Europe, then took a Master's degree from the University of Rochester. He taught at the University of Chicago, in Tehran, and for many years was the Director of the Creative Writing program at NYU. Galway Kinnell was involved over the years in the anti-Vietnam War movement, in movements to support free expression in nations with repressive regimes, in environmental causes and Civil Rights. In 1963, he worked for the Congress of Racial Equality (CORE) registering black voters in Louisiana, which led to his being jailed. He believed that it was the task of poets to bear witness, and said, "To me poetry is somebody standing up so to speak, and saying, with as little concealment as possible, what it is for him or her to be on earth at this moment."

The other unfortunate loss for U.S. poetry is the recent death of Pulitzer Prize winning poet Carolyn Kizer, age 89, on October 9 in Sonoma, California. Born in Spokane, Wa., she was a feminist even back in the 1950s. but unlike Adrienne Rich, as the obit in the *New York Times* put it, where Rich might have flung bombs from the barricades, Kizer's approach was more like a stiletto between the ribs. She took a Bachelor's degree from Sarah Lawrence College, studied Chinese at Columbia University, and later studied poetry with Theodore Roethke and Stanley Kunitz at the University of Washington. She subsequently helped found *Poetry Northwest*, served as its Editor for some 6 years. She taught in Pakistan through a U.S. State Department program, and from 1966-1970 was the first director of literary programs for the National Endowment for the

Arts. She also taught at the University of North Carolina, the Iowa Writer's Workshop and other institutions. In 1998, Kizer and Maxine Kumin resigned as chancellors of the Academy of American Poets to protest the lack of women and minority members. Her second husband, to whom she had been married since 1975, passed away this last June. She was an excellent poet whose work, if you don't know it, you should investigate.

Poet Gary Mex Glazner, of Santa Fe and New York City, the founder of the Alzheimer's Poetry Project and producer of the first National Poetry Slam (San Francisco, 1990), organized a one-day workshop on October 25 in Santa Fe at the History Museum, on Celebrating Creativity in Eldercare. Several organizations sponsored and participated in the event, including Santa Fe poet Stuart Hall. Glazner has been working in this field for some time, producing books of poems by Alzheimer's patients and investigating how poetry helps those who have the disease. This event coincided with Glazner's most recent publication: *Dementia Arts: Celebrating Creativity in Eldercare* (Health Professions Press, 2014).

I want to thank our feature contributors for this issue: Denise Weaver Ross for letting us use her excellent artwork on the covers of this issue. Check out her website, deniseweaverross.com and you can see more of her creations which convert playing card images into artistic entities beyond their original purpose. I also want to thank Portland, Oregon photographer Karen Koshgarian for the photos inside this issue of *MR*, they are outstanding (and thanks to our Pacific Northwest Editor Marilyn Stablein for arranging for our use of these photos). I likewise thank those who helped bring together the feature on Keith Wilson: Heloise Wilson, Lawrence Welsh, and Larry Goodell. I am also grateful for the poems from Nancy Morejón, a poet I have wanted to introduce to *MR* readers for some time. And I want to thank poet Robin MacGowan (and co-translator Reza Saberi) for the feature on Saeb and the ghazals; and, of course MR Associate Editor Dale Harris for her efforts to bring together the huge Feminist anthology. Many thanks to all for making this a rich and diverse issue!

Finally, I want to mention a few new books that I think may be of interest to readers of *MR*: Santa Fe poet John Macker's new book of poems, just issued from Turkey Buzzard Press (Kittredge, Co.), titled *Disassembled Badlands* (118 pp) is an excellent collection of poems that I can recommend. Also, Arthur Sze's 2014 collection of poems *Compass Rose* (Port Townsend, Wa., Copper Canyon Press) is an excellent volume I can easily recommend with enthusiasm. Also, Arthur Sze's 2013 large artbook of poems (and their creative process), in tandem with visual artist Susan York, from Radius Books in Santa Fe titled *The Unfolding Center* (it includes a short interview with Sze and York by John Yau). I am also pleased to recommend Gayle Lauradunn's new book (her first), *Reaching for Air* (Albuquerque, Mercury Heartlink), which is a well written volume about a very negative childhood, rendered in a synthesis of poetic revelation. And John Roche's new (second) anthology of "Joe poems" (the poems all have to say something about someone named Joe), this one titled *Mo' Joe: The Anthology* (Albuquerque, Beatlick Press, 2014, 221 pp).   –GLB

---

*The Harlem Renaissance was an outgrowth of the "New Negro Movement" (a term taken from Alain Locke's 1925 anthology), which also touched the Great African-American Migration from the South to the Midwest and Northeast, to escape the racism and oppression in the South. The "Red Summer" of 1919 was a period of violence in which whites attacked blacks in various locations, for example, killing an estimated 100-200 black sharecroppers in Elaine, Arkansas. The 1920s was also the time of the rise of the Ku Klux Klan in the U.S., in the North as well as in the South. (cf. the Tulsa, Oklahoma, attack on blacks destroyed their section of that city in 1921). In any case, cultural developments in the North, especially in Harlem (NYC) grew with the large influx of southern blacks. Eventually, there was an incredible flowering of the arts there, including poets such as Langston Hughes, Claude McKay, Countee Cullen, prose writers Jean Toomer, Zora Neale Hurston, Alain Locke, James Weldon Johnson, and political activists Marcus Garvey and W.E.B. Dubois, and later James Baldwin. Of course, this eventually included many great jazz and blues musicians, Louie Armstrong, Duke Ellington, Ella Fitzgerald, etc. as well as famous theater and dance folk such as Dorothy Dandridge, Josephine Baker, Bill "Bojangles" Robinson, the Nicolas Brothers and Paul Robeson. Also visual artists listed in the main text.

photo from along old Route 66 by Karen Koshgarian

Hakim Bellamy

A.A. (Afro Anonymous) aka "In Recovery" aka WARdrobe

Remembering Trayvon Martin

"I am an invisible man...I am a man of substance, of flesh and bone, fiber and liquids—and I might even be said to possess a mind. I am invisible, understand, simply because people refuse to see me." —Ralph Ellison (Invisible Man)

Son, if you came up missing
your hood would not be able to find you.
Unable to pick you out in a crowd,
or a police line up.

If you made it that far.
If they even came looking at all.

Don't be anonymous, child.
Make sure you stick out
like a pair of sore thumbs
alongside eight other fingers.
Don't fist.
Don't flinch,
even when their fingers
curl horizontally at your chest.

They won't pull if you don't push,
I pray.

Get em up, high.
As though you could actually reach
those pruned dreams above you,
rotting on each and every branch of government.

Like you're the one being robbed of something,
and everything is suspect.

When standing up for yourself

becomes a crime,
you better stand out.

Like flannel in the summertime.
Like black combat boots and a trench coat
anytime of year.
Like Steven Fuckin' Urkel
pants round your nipples,

or they will put shackles around your ankles.
Hoodies around your neck.
Flowers around your casket.

Because they murder more Stephons
than Steves every single year.

Don't be anonymous, son.
Even if your comrades wear fatigues
every day in this warzone,
and call it a wardrobe,
you rock those plaid shorts
like a Tiger with no stripes
Do not enlist in mortal kombat
with a metropolitan military
that can't see the fathers for the G's,
our future for the trees.

It is open season on hoodies
and skinny jeans.
The only bulletproof vest
I can offer you is beneath
this three-piece suit.
We've worn these neckties for years
because we're least threatening
at the end of a leash.

Speak jive only
as a second language,
because when in Rome

do as conquered people do.

I know…
Romans who?
Empires aren't covered
til long after 1st grade
but it's never too soon to grow up
in this backwards world
of men in backwards hats
getting gunned down in Walmart
for brandishing a toy pistola

While manufacturers live to brand
another day, about how lifelike
their product is…

"So authentic,
even cops can't tell the difference…"

So anonymous,
even cops can't tell the difference.
Son,
this is not cops and robbers
this is cowboys and Indians,
and the only way to not get shot in the back
is to dress like a cowboy.

This poem
is the only arrow pointing you past 19.

When their life
or pride
is in danger,
they cannot tell the difference between you
and the criminal record
they been bumping in their patrol car all day.

The gangsta rap videos
they imagine on loop in your brain

every time you open you mouth
with no "sir."

They can't tell,
just like mothers
trying to identify the mutilated bodies
of their babies.

Pulling Stephon's
personal effects
out of a footlocker
of Air Force Ones
and Phoenix Suns jerseys
like it's a police line up.

I will donate
your carefully creased curb costume
to a "Pimps and Hoes" party
at a fraternity you will never get in
at a college I am determined to get you to
…in one piece

This retired uniform,
designed to help you survive
these gang infested streets
is in need of a facelift.
To help you survive
a more lethal form of thuggery.

Because your tank tops
will never top their tanks.
If wearing a white flag were enough
I would drape you in that,
but it looks too much like the coroner's blanket
and Officer PTSD might mistake you
for a frontline in Iraq.

Take off that bulls eye of conformity, son.
That bullshit dream of equality,

you can't wear whatever you want in this country
that blames women for their own rape
because of what they didn't have on.

You tuck your blackness into your bloodstream
like a white gold chain in the most dangerous part of town,
because the bullets pierce bubble goose parkas
leaving puddles of black boyhood flooding our sewers

And I'm sorry,
but I'd rather have you crying
than leaking
on your way home.

So you will settle
for being the preppiest kid in school.
Wear your culture
like a butt naked emperor.

Like an invisible man.

They will see you when it's convenient,
beyond your Birkenstocks and Brooks Brothers
during the next manhunt.
When boys are fair game.

So, whatever you do
don't be anonymous.

When you go back out to that corner
be the duck wearing a Labrador Retriever costume
in a flock of geese.

At least you know
they won't shoot you, today.
And hey,
if you are lucky,
they might even house break you,
and take you home.

G. L. Brower

Standing My Ground as You Fall on Yours

(For Trayvon Martin, 1995-2012)

"The true racists are the Congressional Black Caucus, the NAACP, and all black leaders..." –Robert Zimmerman (father of George Zimmerman) on Fox News, and a retired Virginia Supreme Court Magistrate.

GeeZee's monologue:

I'm standing my ground
over your dead body
because your existence
caused me to fear you
even though you didn't have a gun
like I did
but I feared
you might do to me
what I did to you,
even though you didn't have a gun,
that you might attack me
like I did you
even though you didn't have a gun
but you had no right to stand
your ground
walk the grass,
run the sidewalk,
defend yourself
like I did,
wear your hoodie in the rain,
because you didn't have a gun,
your doing nothing
was something to me
since you have no right to do anything,
especially since you didn't have a gun,
but I'm your stalker,
not from Neighborhood Watch
but Neighborhood Kill,

because you're only a child,
like so many others I've followed
as the wanna-be cop, my self-appointed job,
you're just another intruding black teen
who didn't have a gun,
has no rights to even walk
the neighborhood,
but now your death is attacking me
when I'm innocent
as the jury my lawyers fooled said,
as the Presiding Judge who helped my defense said,
as my father, the retired Magistrate
and my mother, the ex-court reporter, both said
when they spoke to Sanford Police 44 times,
after they fixed my three previous arrests
for violent confrontations,
after it took 45 days to arrest me,
so now I'm free to shoot anyone
when I feel fear,
when I want to stand my ground,
the elderly with canes,
little boys with toy guns,
women with purses
(you never know what they have in there).
In fact, I feel a threat, a fear,
coming on right now,
so you'd better run,
because I'm untouchable,
invincible, the laws
don't apply to me
because I'm standing my ground
and your ground, and his ground
and her ground and their ground.
So many fears, so little time!
I've got to get at least a couple
of AK-47s.
See, the system works
just fine for me
and I judge people

just like my father did,
only I don't have a gavel,
just my gun,
and you don't.
When I'm holding my gun
it's sexual,
and I love it when I shoot you,
it's like untouchable rapine.
I'm invincible
when confronting the unarmed.
You can say I'm a coward
if you want but I'm not in jail
and the black teen is dead.
No one bites the bullet
like I do,
especially with
the defenseless,
since justice only
applies to everyone else
not me and my gun,
cause my father
was a judge
and yours wasn't.
And you don't have a gun!
Even if you did,
your gun wouldn't kill
my lies,
like my gun
killed you,
killed the truth,
saved the coward in me,
saved my lack of conscience,
saved the vigilante mask
of my face,
as I cut you down
from the lynching tree
in my mind,
where I play games
like the immature man-child I am,

where my tantrums
carry bullets.

Anyway, you don't have a gun,
which means

you're not real.

Christine Eber

Hoodies

come in all colors and sizes
and are good for covering up
when you are cold
or don't want to be noticed.

The young woman from Honduras
tries a green hoodie on her toddler
and asks me why the boy will need it.

I explain it can be cold
on the bus to Atlanta
where her aunt lives
and she'll be on it for a long time,
plus her little boy could use it
when winter comes.

Winter will come for her here
in this land of deferred dreams
because she is one of the lucky ones
who didn't get sent to Artesia,
the 1,000 bed jail for migrants
in Eastern New Mexico.

Instead she came on a school bus
to our cathedral, turned shelter.
Dazed and holding tight
to her toddler's hand,
she decided to believe in us.

We led her into the clothing room
to choose clothes for herself
and her child from the mounds
of donated jeans, t-shirts, jackets,
all sorted by size and gender.
Then she took a shower,

ate her first hot meal in days
and slept.

I imagine her when winter comes to Atlanta,
walking to the corner store for milk and bread.
She'll be glad that her little boy has the hoodie.

I see her pass young men on their way to the store
heads covered in black hoodies,
faces lowered to the sidewalk,
hoping not to be noticed.
These boys could be her brothers
on their way to a neighbor's store
back home in Honduras.
They pray to the Virgin to make it home
before the local gang drags them into their net.

I see her let go of her son's hand
so he can run ahead,
imagine him growing up
in this cold, but hopeful land,
walking with his head up,
free and unafraid.

photo from along old Route 66 by Karen Koshgarian

The Dancer Always Dwells Within:
The Poetry of Keith Wilson
by G. L. Brower

Wilson

"What are politics anyway/but the formalized lusts and greeds of men?"
–Keith Wilson, "The Poem Politic 3"

"Where in America/can you go/that a battle has not been fought/men killed?"
–Keith Wilson, "The Poem Politic 7"

I

The first time I met Keith Wilson (1927-2009), who was maybe the best, or certainly one of the best poets ever to write in and about New Mexico, it was 1970, maybe 1971. I had moved here to teach at UNM. Shortly after that my friend, poet Vic Contoski, a colleague at Kansas University where I had previously taught, came down to visit and asked to be taken to meet Keith Wilson. I didn't know who Keith was then. (My specialty was Latin American poetry/essay; I was a professor in the Spanish Department, and had only recently begun to write my own poetry in English.) The fact that Vic knew who he was, indicated that Keith's fame reached beyond his home state. And I trusted Vic's judgment. I immediately made plans for us to drive down to Las Cruces. Later, I made it a point to read as many of Keith's published poems as possible around my readings in Hispanic literatures. And what I found is that if you want to know New Mexico, its culture and history, through poetry, Keith's work is a great way to do it.

Born in Clovis, raised in the Ft. Sumner area, a long-time professor at NMSU in Las Cruces, Keith was the quintessential 20th Century poet of the state. Said another way, Keith was probably the best anglo poet of the state in his time, because his purview included Hispanic and Native American cultures, as well as the role of History and the importance of Nature. He brought them all together in the context of personal experience: growing up in pastoral New Mexico of the 1930s, critter branding, rattlers, horses, local cowboy characters, farm/ranch-life and so many other adventures. His poems give us narratives, almost mini-novels, of how it was back then, and in some places still is. He brings together the synthesis of Culture with the Analysis of History in just a few words. But he's not just a poet of the past, he's a poet for all time.

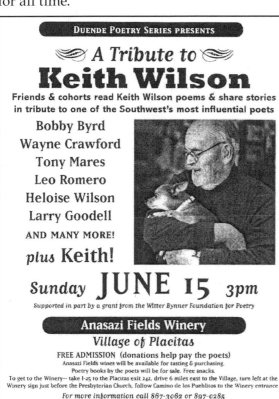

DUENDE POETRY SERIES PRESENTS

≈ A Tribute to ≈

Keith Wilson

Friends & cohorts read Keith Wilson poems & share stories in tribute to one of the Southwest's most influential poets

Bobby Byrd
Wayne Crawford
Tony Mares
Leo Romero
Heloise Wilson
Larry Goodell
AND MANY MORE!

plus Keith!

Sunday JUNE 15 3pm

Supported in part by a grant from the Witter Bynner Foundation for Poetry

Anasazi Fields Winery
Village of Placitas

FREE ADMISSION (donations help pay the poets)
Anasazi Fields wines will be available for tasting & purchasing.
Poetry books by the poets will be for sale. Free snacks.
To get to the Winery— take I-25 to the Placitas exit 242, drive 6 miles east to the Village, turn left at the
Winery sign just before the Presbyterian Church, follow Camino de los Pueblitos to the Winery entrance
For more information call 867-3062 or 897-0285

And there was the last time I saw Keith. A tribute reading was held in his honor on June 15, 2008, at the Anasazi Fields Winery in Placitas, home of the Duende Poetry Series. A large number of poets came together from all over the state and beyond, especially from southern New Mexico, to read for Keith. He was seriously ill, and rather than wait to have a tribute for him after his demise, the idea was to honor him while he could appreciate it. He had had a stroke and couldn't speak, though he understood everything. Heloise, his wife and fellow poet, spoke for him, read some of his poems, and some of her own too. It was a good-bye to Keith, one we didn't want to acknowledge, but had to. It was a stanza we all wrote that poetic day for him. It was about letting Keith go (but not quite yet). It was a great reading in which we remembered his enduring poetry. It was a gathering of poets to honor the excellence of New Mexico's best poetic son. It was a moment in which we wanted to build a protective wall of metaphors and words around Keith, a foolish gesture but which we had the "poetic license" to do anyway. Perhaps it was an attempt to use metaphor as a weapon against death. And, in all actuality, it was simply a way of honoring a poet important to us.

Keith was never published by UNM Press, but was (I think) the first New Mexico bard to have a book of poems (*Graves Registry*) nominated for the National Book Award for Poetry. He could have been the state's Poet Laureate if there had been such a position. We wanted to let him know how much he was appreciated, and we hope we did so. Heloise assured us this was the case. Keith passed away on February 10, 2009. But, as we know, his work lives on, and needs to be read. That is the point of this feature.

Last year, I went on a trip to Asia: Cambodia/Angkor Wat, Vietnam, South Korea. In our short time in Seoul, where we took a day-tour, my memory kicked in and I began to feel reverberations from the past, especially about my dad's experiences in the U.S. Army in the Korean War in the 1950s. And I thought of Keith and his experiences, as expressed in his poems in *Graves Registry*, in that same war, now a mostly forgotten conflict except in Korea.

And then my memory brought back that reading for Keith in Placitas in 2008. When it was my turn to read, I chose the second half of a funerary poem for my dad, who had passed away in 2007 and who had returned from his military tour in Korea via Japan. In more than one poem, Keith refers to the famous/infamous (but ubiquitous) Japanese song "China Nights." This catchy tune, called *Shinanoyoru* in Japanese and sung by a young woman, most Korean War vets would recall. It was actually an imperialistic tune from the days when Japan invaded China, and it celebrated that imperialism, which the GIs didn't know since it was sung in Japanese. Keith mentions the song in two or three poems, e.g. in "Combat Mission":

> While fires flickered on the hills
> they went, confident, out into the night
> where heavy weapons grumbled
> & a Korean boy played "China Night"
> on a squeaky phonograph... (p. 31, *Graves Registry*)*

Another poem carried the title "China Night" (I've never figured out whether the song title should be singular or plural), and notes that U.S. soldiers parodied the song, which they didn't understand, singing "I ain't got no yo-o-yo," which sounds a little like one line of the Japanese lyrics.[1] It's amazing in a way how the human mind works. In this case, one thin, high-voiced song relating two eras and the experiences of two men who never met, from the same war, funneled through my mind to Keith's poems, with the same reference. Part I of my poem for my father, titled "The Music Box," describes his death in a hospital bed, as we watched, helpless, and Part II is as follows:

> Weeks later, my mother and I sort through
> my father's tangible memories, intangible objects,
> discover a wooden music box, carved owl on the front,
> bought in return transit from the Korean War.
>
> My mother says the box long ago lost its music
> which he tried to coax out many times
> before finally storing the voiceless memento
> in catacombs of the past.
>
> But as I open the box, reflected in the little mirror
> inside the lid, it starts playing it's one-song repertoire-
> as if a tiny amnesiac orchestra had suddenly awakened
> to play the famous *China Nights*, shocking us back
> into another era.
>
> In our stark, sudden startle, we think

of this tinny tune as my father's voice
from the Other Side of the Past.

We picture him walking into a Japanese souvenir shop,
circa 1951, where he finds his later ethereal voice
in the midst of hundreds of human and animal-shaped
        clocks,
all eyes back and forth in left-right timely tick-tock,
a disorienting vision of mass ocular movement,
while all music boxes tinkled their songs
in a distorted cacophony of notes.

He picks out the three-color wooden box,
leaves the vertigo of the shop,
opens the lid to see his eyes uncross
in the little mirror, hears *Shinanoyoru*
which he whistles while he walks,
looking both ways, like an owl,
before crossing the street
into the military base at Camp Sasebo.[2]

Keith's war poems are always included in considerations of
poetry of the Korean War (1950-53), along with a number of other
poets, some very good, some quite famous. What's interesting
about this is that the war itself is not well remembered (a monu-
ment to the veterans of the conflict was dedicated on the Mall
in Washington, D.C. 42 years later), and so poetry about it is
similarly not so well known. Not many know about the "Poetry
of the Korean War," just as the "Poetry of the Vietnam War" has
now generally been forgotten. But the fact is casualties from the
Korean War were approximately 40,000 American troops dead,
100,000 wounded, within a general total of 5 million military
and civilians dead. And there were quite a number of poets who
wrote about the conflict.

One of the uncommon status problems may be that legally
the war was called a United Nations' "Police Action" and only
later did it become the "Korean War." (Twenty-some nations sent

troops to create the UN armed forces in Korea.) In the context of the "Cold War" of that time,[3] the only reason the conflict actually happened was that a vote of the UN Security Council was allowed to declare it because the Russian delegate Anastas Mikoyan, as I recall, walked out of the meeting in protest rather than veto the proposal (a mistake never repeated by the Russians). As a UN operation, the goal was to stop the complete takeover of the Korean peninsula by the Chinese-trained North Koreans, and defend South Korea, which, under authoritarian, right-wing President Syngman Rhee, was aligned with the WWII Western Powers (U.S., Britain, France, etc.). When Kim Il Sung's 75,000- man North Korean Army crossed the 38th Parallel (the bi-national boundary) on June 25, 1950, the war was on. The Cold War got Hot! But almost as soon as it started, efforts to defuse the war were underway because of the danger of either a nuclear war or WWIII. The complication was that this was a UN operation and not just two nations in battle, but with large military powers in the background, i.e. the U.S. and Russia.

For me, the "turning point" poem in *Graves Registry* is "Corsair" where Keith recounts the death of a friend who returns to an air carrier–and doesn't make it–right there before his eyes:

> It was of course Don
> who died. (...)

> At full roar, one by
> one they returned.

> Minus him.

> It was of course of course
> my friend

>> in the twisted aluminum
>> the shining spars
>> crumpled wheels (....)

35

It was of course he
who refused, who would not
kill, would not obey, would
not return–refused

to machinegun civilians
on the Korean hillside
to bomb a courtyard
full of refugees

It was I on the bridge
of the carrier, waiting
counting the planes–marked
the return of the squadron leader,
he who taught him that

low, slow turn
just above stalling speed
the fighter's controls mush
there, aces away from a spin

He spun. He lay
there and I of course
wait, wait for whatever
second coming there can be
for a splattered flyer
my friend, lying there

who would not kill idly (....)
(*Graves Registry*, pp. 128-129)

This poem joins Keith's anecdotal/personal experience to the larger collective of military history. This little death-movie, through his perfect description and minimal but powerful words about the death of a friend, portrays an incident repeated more than once in the Korean War. It was a footnote for the U.S. Navy, with its grandiose context of the larger war, but for Keith this was obviously the macro come down to the micro, into a pinpoint focus of what war comes down to in the end, the death of many of its participants. He makes the reader feel what he felt, demands the reader feel the demise of his friend. You know his emotions, feelings, mind, twisted together to focus on the mortal drama. He sees his friend glide down into his death. And he tells you why he (and you as reader) should care: because he was a friend, he was a caring pilot, he refused to bomb innocent civilians. And he pays the ultimate price, while other pilots who may not have cared so much about humanity, who only followed orders without thinking, survived. It brings up the question of justice in death, always there, but especially in war. It is war's time and space: we project into space, the distance of Keith on the bridge and the pilot on the carrier deck below, and into time, that moment when it ended for the returning flyer. That moment is like the vanishing point in a painting, it's where the reader's consciousness vanishes into the poem. Then we focus back on the poet, and Keith describes his own vanishing point, as his friend lay there, now a corpse. This is one of the most powerful poems about war I can recall. You see it unfold through the poet's eyes as it happens. A sort of play-by-play of death.

Keith's family had an extensive military tradition (see his mini-autobiography toward the end of *Shaman of the Desert*). True to it, he graduated from the U.S. Naval Academy in Annapolis, Maryland. A man of high, dry desert background was thrust out onto the great expanse of the ocean, perhaps a sort of anti-desert, with seaweed instead of cholla. But what Keith saw and experienced turned him into an anti-war poet. The best wartime poets put the reader into the battle, into the terrible experience of violence or its consequences, and this Keith does very, very well. Certainly in "Corsair" and in many other poems, he could see everything with his binoculars. In "Memory of a Victory," he tells of looking at the Korean coast beyond Wonsan, "a picture world with low hills/much like New Mexico." He notes, "the planes still had not come, all eternity/waited beneath the sweep second hand." Then, "...the crackling radio commanded/ Fire! and a distant world I could have loved/went up in shattering bursts."

(p. 122). In "The Circle," Keith writes of being in the Yellow Sea 20 miles off Inchon, when his ship moves into an area where it is surrounded by floating bodies of dead soldiers, "Most of the men leaned/back, heads bobbing against/kapok collars, mouths open,/tongues swollen/ –hundreds of them..." (pp. 16-17). We are experiencing these events on the human (or inhuman) level, on Keith's level rather than on the level of a General or Admiral. In another poem, "Commentary," he sees bodies being lined up on a beach as he floats by onboard his vessel. Perhaps as an extension of the combat poems, there are also those which address the larger questions of war and peace. In "Hiroshima," he brings the tragedy of the atomic blast down to specific focus on one person, a "Japanese girl": "I speak the word {Hiroshima} & see/-oval eyes, a burned cheek,/trace the scars/with shaking fingers." (p. 34).

To put Keith's combat poetry into a slightly larger context, that of "Korean War Poetry by American veterans," it's clear that he's one of the major poets of that sub-genre. Other U.S. poets of note who were in that war or wrote about it include William Meredith, Hayden Carruth, Tom McGrath (with his "Ode for the American dead in Korea" from his *Selected Poems*), and one of the most famous Chicano poet-novelists of all time, Rolando Hinojosa,[4] This award-winning writer says, in his Korean War poem "Friendly Fire": "Light travels faster than sound/but sound travels fast enough for some. /the burned hand caught the shrap direct and sailed off/...the hip too felt the smoking clumps.../...'raise those sights, Sergeant Kell,' /the forward ob says, 'you're still short'," (from Hinojosa's *Korean Love Songs*). Yes, in war, violence has its casualties among friend and foe alike. A "Korean War veteran for peace" (as he describes himself), Woody Powell, in "Man in Uniform" says that all who suffer in war have their spirit distorted: "I am a man/....A spirit swollen, diseased,/ infected by Colt, Browning and Boeing,/with the awesome power of death." (from Powell's book with Zhou Ming-fu, *Two walk the Golden Road*). This is why poets have to repair themselves by their art, if they can, and others too, if possible. This is why their poems can often be cathartic to write, read.

II

Keith Wilson's poetry is most known for his stories about New Mexico, its history, his experiences from rural childhood in the 1930s, his relationships with the Hispanic and Indian populace who form the majority of the state's people.[5] As heartfelt as his Korean War poems are, it's the appeal of New Mexico's land, cultures and nature that comprise the bedrock of Keith's memory and poetry, from childhood to maturity, in a time-warp from the Past that takes you back to that history through the power of his poems. In "Stampede" (p. 11) he brings you into the action:

> I'd done it, ridden too fast
> past spooky cattle, massed and restless, and they
> ran, shaking the narrow wash, crushing calves under
> their hooves, two weeks good grass vanishing.

And if you've seen a western film, you know what they had to do–rush to the head of the stampede and turn the lead steer to turn the cattle:

> The foreman and I cut outward by instinct, riding hard,
> the leather creaking, my horse's breath coming in
> hard grunts, ...

Once they were able to turn the steers and get them back in the arroyo, Keith recalls the last step in quieting the critters:

> A boy and a man, on horses. And what
> it felt like to walk that horse slowly back and forth across
> the mouth of that draw. Waving yellow slickers and crying
> softly, "Ho boy, Ho there!" in loving voices, in quietly tensed
> voices....

Besides critters, there were old coots out there too, such as he describes in "The Rancher,":

> Hard old grey eyes, no pity in him
> after years of branding cattle–
> a cruel man with cows & men
>
> he drove both hard & once
> when he was 70 tried to kill
> a young puncher for smiling at his
>
> old wife, sat down & cried in fury
> because his grown sons took his
> ivory handled .45 away, held
>
> his head in his arms & didn't
> ever come back to the dance.
> After a while his wife went slowly
>
> out into the clear night
> saying how late it is getting
> now isn't it?.....

Keith has so many poems that are little vignettes of rural life in the 1930s. Together they form a picture of those times and places, with characters, anecdotal history mixed with collective history sometimes, events on the ground, legends. They are often story-poems talking about real people and occurrences. In "Birdey Riley & Brother: Rustlers," Keith tells us what happened in 1909 in New Mexico Territory. The two brothers were out riding, and as they were in the process of rustling Jesús Montoya's horses in a storm, Birdey's brother is struck and killed by lightning:

> ....Birdey & his brother pushed
> the stolen horses slowly back into the draw
> kicking their own mounts down the stone trail.

–a flash, a bolt of light no bigger
than a fencepost hit Birdey's brother
on top of the head, burned through him,

the horse & left wet grass smoking. Birdey
shifted in the saddle, watched the rain put
out the smoldering fires in his brother's clothes,

his hair, then slowly he rode back to town letting
the horses go....went to tell
the undertaker where to find his brother.
He paid the man, rode off, not even changing
his clothes. Later he wrote for some gear.

He was a Baptist preacher by then, called
himself "Richard." (....)   (p. 165)

Another poem involves the Penitente religious sect [6] which existed from the later Spanish colonial period until today. Their practice of reenacting the crucufixion, and the sect itself, were prohibited by the Roman Catholic Church for many years. But this narrative is real. By tradition, the person chosen for Penitente "crucifixion" found an empty pair of shoes at his door. "Teófilo's Father" (pp. 170-171) tells of the ritual death of one sect member who "takes the place of Christ."

Teófilo's father
died on the cross at Easter
a Penitente, chosen,
brought in his young
manhood
to the *morada* & beaten
the Wounds of Christ, one
by one they pierced him.

He marched in the
procession.

41

Men, carrying whips, lashed
Him & each other up the
rocky Hill. They tied Him on
the Cross, raised it, tamped
the dark earth firm.

Later, after a vigil, they cut him down and carried him
through the streets of the village for three days "until the smell
drove all but the devout away." Finally, says Keith, "my father, his
friend, put the tarp-wrapped body in his pickup," drove it all the
way to Anton Chico.

Keith's two poems that focus on Billy the Kid, that iconic
outlaw of New Mexico, are both very different than, say, Michael
Ondaatje's famous *The Collected Works of Billy the Kid* (my 1970
copy is from Norton in New York). They tell Billy's story–warts
and all. One is "Trio: Billy the Kid" (pp. 180-184), and the other
is "The Lincoln County War" (pp. 299-300). In the first poem, he
presents Billy's history of crime (thievery, horse rustling, shoot-
ing down lawmen, etc.) and then his personality, popularity with
the Mexican people in the state (among whom he was known as
el chivato–the little goat), numerous girlfriends, his gun (a Colt
.38), his penchant for escaping jails. He went by several surnames:
Antrim, Bonney, McCarty, this last apparently the name on his
Indiana birth certificate (1859). Denied clemency for various
crimes by Lew Wallace (New Mexico Territorial Governor, former
Union General, author of *Ben Hur*), he was eventually killed by
Sheriff Pat Garrett (an ambush inside a house, from behind a bed)
in Ft. Sumner (1881). The Kid's cohorts, Bowdre and O'Foliard,
were killed there too and buried with him. He was mainly
known as Billy the Kid later, when his story was embellished
and published in pamphlets and books by popularizers trying
to make a buck. Keith's second poem on the Lincoln County
War synthesizes that conflict between greedy money-grubbers
Tunstall and McSween and Billy's participation, bringing it on
past the historical reality into the era of old retired gunmen.
In general terms, many feel that Billy wasn't quite so bad until
Governor Wallace, who had promised him a quid pro quo pardon

but reneged, led to Billy's change to a "bad guy." In any case, Billy became an outlaw icon. And Keith presents him both "in the good and in the bad."

In "Poem for the Mountain Gods" (pp.309-12) Keith talks about Mescalero Apache ceremonials as he attends a dance–the drumming, devil dancers, Gan dancers,[7] the brush wickiups,[8] the big fire, the bright blankets around the women, leaping male dancers, women slowly circling. And he has a number of poems about the town of San Miguel where he and Heloise lived for a time, the people, traditions and nature of that small Hispanic town. If you add up all of these poems, and there are a lot more, it tells you a lot about New Mexico on a very real level–the dances, the quarrels, the courting, gardens, farming, ranching, herding wild horses, etc. History is always near the surface of any current reality in New Mexico; this is true of Keith' poetry about the state too. In his poem "In New Mexico Territory, as best as I can understand" (p. 437), Keith comments on one transition (which implies the process of change itself), the changeover from the 19th Century into the 20th Century:

> It all began with men, and with women
> edging, nudging them on. Perhaps the horses
>
> were partly to blame, the killings sent the horses
> wild, they danced on their white stockinged feet
>
> in their great eyes gunfire flashed and rolled.
> Now we have all this. The gunfighters still hold
>
> the cities and some of the towns. The horses are
> mostly gone and it is the land that is dying.
>
> My coyote friends and I sit separate in darkness
> watching the winking lights, we remember.

When you read Keith's poems, you see what has been lost, or perhaps we should say "changed." And you see how an excellent poet can bring that process to you in poems. How such a poet can put your life in the perspective of the place, and from different angles. And show how New Mexico is unique in the U.S. and the world. Keith Wilson became the poet of our reality, both past and present. In the mosaic of his work, each piece joins to form the picture of who we are, were, and might be–but only if we don't discard that which makes us unique.

NOTES

1 This poem is from p.6 of Keith's book *Graves Registry* (Livingston, Mt., Clark City Press, 1992). All quotes in Part I of his essay are from this edition and all page indications throughout are the same.

2 Camp Sasebo=An American military base in Japan. This poem was published in *Adobe Walls, No. 4, pp. 74-76.*

3 The term "Cold War" was a state of political and military tension after the "Hot War' of WWII, between the U.S. and its NATO allies and the Soviet Union and the Warsaw Pact. Some say it lasted from 1947-1991.

4 Rolando Hinojosa (b. 1929) is a major Chicano poet, novelist and essayist. His poems about his time in the military during the Korean War are found in his *Korean Love Songs* (1978). His prose works won the *Casa de Las America* Prize from the Cubans as well as the *Quinto Sol* Prize.

5 All quotes/page references in Part II of this essay are from Keith's complete poetic works, *Shaman of the Desert* (Livingston, Mt., Clark City Press, 2009), 1104 pp.

6 The Penitente sect was a "lay confraternity" based in northern New Mexico and southern Colorado among the Hispanic populace and was not approved by the Catholic Church until modern days. It was founded in the early 19th Century when the church's staffing in the area was sparse, so the faithful carried on their religious practices. Today it is a benevolent association for its members.

7 Gan dancers=Western Apache dancers who are supposed to represent the mountain spirits.

8 Wickiup=A brush-constructed dome house, especially associated with Apache tribes.

G. L. Brower

To A Desert Shaman

For Keith Wilson, 1927-2009

"Poetry comes at truth full on, but from an angle."
– Octavio Paz.

His poems have rhythmic feet
at the Stanza Harvest Dance.

He whirls them around
till their feet leave the floor.

He felt the flow of words
down acequias of the mind–

an offering of metaphors
to the Four Directions,
sacred poetic pollen in the wind.

Hunched mountains,
petrified dinosaur-backs,
lurk in the epic distance
that lyrically seem much closer.

Coyotes & bears
roadrunners & prairie dogs
jackrabbits & wolves
deer & elk
lizards & old coots
brought him words.

Here and there
desert springs of syllables
burst forth
in hidden canyons.

45

The shaman
drank deep–
traced truth
in the sand
with the rattle
of a sidewinder.

Goodell on Keith Wilson

by Larry Goodell

I
Shaman of the Desert

Goodell

Keith Wilson's *Shaman of the Desert, Collected Poems (1965-2001)* is a massive volume of over 1100 pages containing works from at least a couple dozen of his books.

Drum Hadley, long-time friend of Keith Wilson's, says in his introduction to this *Collected*, "it seems like we have always known each other. I went to the University of Arizona and I met him right off. I said I was interested in writing poetry and people told me, 'see Keith Wilson.' It was the beginning of what has become a lifelong friendship and creative exchange." And in Las Cruces where the Wilsons moved to, they continued to be "a gathering place, creating a community made of words, ideas, and dreams— where many a young poet was nourished by their good food and company." And the books of poetry kept coming, subject to the ups and downs of small press publishing, so this *Collected* from Clark City Press can be your Keith Wilson bible. As Hadley says in his Introduction, "Wilson's poetry is raw and honest. What is inessential has been pared away, only intensifying it's impact. Keith describes his writings as 'Emotional Geography.' He guides the reader through transformational terrain, reacquainting them with a deeper place within the self."

I can't begin to be in any way comprehensive about this incredibly moving and extensive achievement, but I can bring together here two reviews I did of two of his books, *Lion's Gate*, 1986, and *Graves Registry*, 1992. Also here are a couple short statements about the importance of Keith's work to me. We were born about a hundred miles apart and he was only eight years older than me but *he was always my New Mexican elder.* And I include a poem of his I picked almost at random, but it nevertheless expresses that honest grit representative of the poet's best work. At the end of this essay I include the poem I wrote after his death.

I've had these lines of Keith Wilson's on my study wall, now almost unreadable from paper disintegration, the last three lines central in many ways:

. . .

> "& all the time,
> *Nuestro Señor,*
>
> there was this song
> all about me
> it had only to open
> my mouth to sing."

And from last line of "New Mexico: *Paso Por Aqui*" I quote, "All men are visitors here."

II
Keith Wilson, New Mexico's Leading Poet: 1988
This youthful review of Lion's Gate, Selected Poems 1963-1986 *by Keith Wilson (Cinco Puntos Press, El Paso) first appeared in Southwestern Discoveries, June-August 1988, in my column Backfire.*

Lion's Gate roars in the face of the Yuppie invasion of New Mexico as the Peugeots and Saabs pull up to the Post Office and people lock their cars there for the first time in history. The wind hits the coiffures and business suits and that, simply, in Spring, is New Mexico reclaiming its history. The wind hits hard: death, the odd, the tough, the ghosts, the desert is hard.

These are "stories." Call them "poems" if you like. Stories make up the history of this man's art which is poetry. You can theorize poetry to death, break it up into compartments and whisk it away. Or make an icon of it and install it in the University to assure you and your buddies of a job. You can be a non-language poet, a langoiterage poet, a New American Regionalist poet: all these things are a crock, because anything with strength and individuality transcends borders, definitions, crocks.

Lion's Gate is real, real-ler than a dozen Milagro Beanfield Wars in substance and song and authenticity. Would that Keith Wilson could be touted and read as much, but not adored beyond reason and eaten up in the American Video Machine.

A poem is an utterance of a new-old: the language older, the voice of the poet the newer. And to read *Lion's Gate* from cover to cover is hearing a man revealed. There's the mother, the father, the relatives. "The Arrival of My Mother" is the archetypal Western Expansion poem to me. And there is in Wilson the place in a way that stomps through Western reruns and strangles everything to get to the source: that is, the immaterial, the second rate, the bullshit falls off like dross: the Western *in original dressing* is revealed.

There's an encounter with *deja vu*, more than that, reincarnation actuallized as we travel instantly back in "The Minaret At Constanta" to a lion's gate in Rumania– the Western Expansion retraced through the intense darkness and voice of the Poet Deluxe.

There is the reinvigorated power of the revealed poet. Layers come off and I don't mean clothes, the history sings through verse, through the energy that mouths sing and have sung, told, laid down and storyized, *where all is never all told*: gaps create the poem's imagination, the reader/listener is vitalized in reenacting the real poet, as Keith Wilson is.

Among the many works as "Midwatch," "Seacaptain," and "Chantey," there are perhaps the best Korean War poems that have come to light: the section from *Graves Registry.* They make you think of Wilfred Owen's First World War atrocities, and Viet Nam revealed by Larry Rottman in *Winning Hearts and Minds,* and the many that have followed him. But the sea and war travel return to "know that my desert is a condition of soul / not topography. It is where one wrestles with devils / and knows they are oneself." – from "Chantey"

In 1988, I wrote this in "Teachers," a series of short poems:

49

Keith Wilson–
he was the old voice
the bear voice in newest everyday now,
he taught me to bear with it and it
will tell the story.

III

This review of Graves Registry *by Keith Wilson (Clark City Press) appeared in*
Blue Mesa Review, Spring 1993:

This collection, a Keith Wilson magnum opus, brings together
what Grove Press did in 1969 *(Graves Registry and Other Poems)* and
what Sumac Press did in 1972 *(Midwatch),* and adds about 50 pieces
to make up a handsome 216 page edition from Clark City Press in
Montana. Things have been clarified: poems that were just num-
bered before are now titled, there are certain additions and resto-
rations, but the major parts have remained as Keith Wilson wrote
them, in high heat. You have the obvious proportions of an epic
on war, a book poem that allows the poet to play out the human
species' obsession with war. You could say it's Keith Wilson's ob-
session, but when you reach the end and pass through "the battle-
fields of galaxies" you realize the truth of his hammering and the
shield of this book becomes timeless, Homeric, and present. Look
at what's happening, *now,* 1993: war is part of us.

Graves Registry is *a poem.* (The cover of this beautiful publica-
tion erringly refers to the work as "poems.") The most graphic
parts come at the very beginning in "Korea-Japan, 1950-53," and
echo the much earlier poet Wilfred Owen in their depictions of
death. Subsequent sections are like shock waves recalling those
things experienced in action. The Young Lieutenant seems to be
the poet's persona, antipathetic to the Sea Captain, who figures
strongly as the poem progresses.

I think of Dante's *Inferno,* but more of the conversations
through space of Milton's *Paradise Lost.* I think of Wilfred Owen,
and especially Benjamin Britten's *War Requiem:* I can hear it back-
ing Owen's genius depiction of death and that lie "Dulce et deco-
rum est pro patria mori." These are evoked in me, reading *Graves*

Registry. But mostly, I think of the great Charles Olson's *Maximus Poems.* For instance here is the beginning of Olson's "Maximus, to Himself,"

> I have had to learn the simplest things
> last. Which made for difficulties.
> Even at sea I was slow, to get the hand out, or to cross
> a wet deck.
> > The sea was not, finally, my trade.
> But even my trade, at it, I stood estranged
> from that which was most familiar.

Here is a piece from "A Masque for the Warriors, Home," the last part of Wilson's *Graves Registry.*

Antistrophe

> All the voices spin down, lost
> beyond whatever recall the memories
> of lives lived and died, held briefly
> to glints of moonlight, crowns that crumble.
>
> There is left the counting of graves.
> The slash of swordblade an epitaph
> shudder of cannon in circling echoes
>
> the bones rot within the ring,
> boys' faces kiss shadow girls
> rings rings around Saturn or Mars

Graves Registry is a grandiose work, unnerving, troubling, obsessive, powerful, relentless, visionary, comprehensive, bold and musical. It is an immense and tragic poem that both includes and transcends boundaries of space and time. It ultimately *succeeds,* and what a pleasure that New Mexico's greatest poet has not only received the Governor's Award for excellence in the arts, but now has this important work at last available from Clark City

51

Press in Montana. What I and many others regret is that our own University of New Mexico Press stubbornly refuses to publish the rich store of New Mexico poets. What a miss! Keith Wilson is from Fort Sumner and is a resident of Las Cruces where he has taught and worked for years. His works should be fully available and in print, since this poet is a living treasure of our state and our country.

IV

I wrote this in my notebook in 2000:

No poet writes with such gristle and grace as Keith Wilson who in Bosque Redondo excites again the pleasure of what it's like to be a true New Mexican, a voice of this hard land that sings from the depths as well as the shallows. No poet so truthfully evokes the real world that includes the ancients in the gritty day-to-day living in our own home state.

Opening *Shaman of the Desert* you'll find many poems such as this one from *While Dancing Feet Shatter the Earth*.

The Voices of My Desert

Beginning this new trail, with the resonance
of shifting earth about me, I hear calls
distancing the crow voices of my childhood,

the wolf cry of my middle age. The sun
is an ancient symbol above me and God knows
what the mountains, spirit blue on the horizon

mean. Silence stands within me as without
desert stirs to its own subtle communication.
There is time, always, to wonder, doubt.

New Mexico is a myth, an ancient whirlpool
of time where moments stand still just before
being sucked down to other planes, other hours.

We hold time back through rituals, dances
that stir the seconds like flecks of sand
beneath our feet, eternities of the possible.

I write down the words I hear, but I know
it is the Dead who speak them. Our ears
are tuned to the past, hear, hear the days

less clearly than the flute-songed nights
with their last owls whitefaced as moons
swooping low for the poisoned, dying mice.

The ghosts of wolves ring our hills.
Those birdcries, Comanche songs drifting
up from wartrails: the click of steel

in the night, prospectors or old soldiers
sharpening the edge of darkness to a keen
wind that blows all the stories away.

    He says "I write down the words I hear, but I know / it is the Dead who speak them." As the voices of the past inform the voices of the present, Mr. Wilson's voice is prominent among them.

Shaman of the Desert is available in hardback, $40, and in paper, $30. Query Heloise Wilson: kewilson@zianet.com, or email me: larrygood@ comcast.net

Larry Goodell

Keith

(1927-2009)

Who more than you opens doors to where we live?
and we live here whether Las Cruces, Albuquerque
      Santa Fe Taos Roswell Fort Sumner,
          and where in this so-called Southwest,
who more than you breathes the past with the present?
Who tells the story more than you and
      punctuates it with a laugh
or brings the mystery out in the open
to be pondered and wondered at?
where the multifaceted multi-ethnic trans-animal
      trans-person melt into the specifics
         of the story of each act
      which is the reality of living here you get at
and release to us to see what is right before our eyes.
Your voice excites the present with place, places
      faces animal and plant and dry presence,
story after story that comes up out of the arroyos
and brings the past with it, the ancients
      the voices breaking out of caves
         or from their graves
to face us in your family land, your love
of this earth here you articulate father mother
son daughters wife friends strangers
to introduce us, amused, carried on in words
      your voice brings me face to face
         with where I live

Mortality, Immortality and the Resurrection of Keith Wilson

by Lawrence Welsh

Welsh

When a city's most important writer dies, does that city die too? That's the question I often ask with regard to Las Cruces, New Mexico, and Keith Wilson.

Wilson, a native New Mexican who was born in Clovis in 1927, died in 2009. For many in the know, he remains one of the state's greatest poets, and after spending more than 40 years in Las Cruces and Southern New Mexico, he became known as "The Shaman of the Desert."

That, of course, is an almost impossible tag to live up to, but Wilson embodied every aspect of the title while never acknowledging it. He simply was, for many, the definitive New Mexican, one who channeled the landscape directly through his blood and into his love for the people and the language of the Southwest.

Perhaps his poems were molded by Spanish, his first language. Maybe they came about because he carried, and proudly so, Celtic and Irish blood. Whatever the reasons, we're lucky that in 2009 Clack City Press in Livingston, Montana, published the massive, 1,100 page *Shaman of the Desert: The Collected Poems of Keith Wilson, 1965-2001.*

Wilson never saw the book's completion, but he knew of its progress and talked proudly of its forthcoming publication. Like the equally massive *Collected Poems of Ted Hughes*, Wilson's final omnibus reads like an homage to both the seen and unseen worlds, a calling out to spirits that have inhabited this earth for centuries and can no longer be visited by the living. Like Hughes, the words and images seemed to arrive orally, long before words ended up on paper or parchment. Of course Wilson didn't have Hughes' luck, and his *Shaman Collected* received scant notice upon its arrival. It didn't help that Wilson was already dead, and it didn't improve chances for success when Clark City Press went broke soon after Wilson's publication. In the end, the book never went out for review or award consideration. The publisher, a well-known artist who put out beautiful books, simply closed and moved back to Northern California to devote the rest of his life to painting.

The massive tome then slipped into obscurity with little recognition at all. And Wilson, too, has mostly been forgotten. In fact, nowadays many Southwest writers have no idea of his work or worth. One too would suspect that Google could deliver a vast amount of "hits" about his life and backlog. Sadly, that isn't the case. In the end, Wilson has become like the desert itself: capable of turning into only dust, sand and wind. In some way, I know he wouldn't mind this. Some 40 mostly out of print volumes are still out there, and the collected is available for anyone who wants to dig it up. Only time will tell what sort, if any, resurrection will occur. Without doubt, though, Wilson deserves a generous one.

Stepping back a bit, I remember first encountering Wilson's work in 1994, when I permanently moved to El Paso from Los Angeles. On many occasions, he wound up in El Paso at a wide range of readings: lofts, parties and loose get-togethers. He had already secured his place as one of the masters of the area, and I had difficulty relating to his work, mainly because I was still immersed in an L.A. existence of pure urbanism: steel, concrete, smog, gang wars, constant racism, those sort of things.

About a year later, I immersed myself in a new life by taking long solo hikes into the Chihuahuan Desert, both in West Texas and Southern New Mexico. I also started praying and meditating in the desert. Somehow, I remembered Wilson's work and returned to his books. It's not a misnomer to say that they came alive anew, and the words gave credence to the physical and spiritual landscapes. Certainly, the Catholicism I grew up with was transfigured and rearranged in Wilson's words, but one also sensed a channeling of both Celtic and Native American worlds.

Around this time I called, and he invited me into his home. On those trips, I always took a notebook, so I could listen and write down whatever recommendations he would make.

In his first chapbook, *Sketches for a New Mexican Hill Town*, published in 1965, Wilson set the stage for the rest of his poetic career, by remembering the sacred world of "Los Penitentes," that devout lay order of New Mexico Catholic men.

> of the needs of men,
> backs raw from cactus whips
> yet speaking of light, they who were
> Brothers of Light, brown men
>   chanting
>
> Humble Christs,
> singing
> to the agonies o
> of wounds...

Perhaps, then, too, the poem becomes a portrait not only of the rigors of the spiritual life, but the life that Wilson would live – that of the poet: "Smoking & flaming/through the tall grass, after/ all these years, it is the/darkness they left behind."

As with any great poet, however, darkness eventually turns to light, and the desert light of New Mexico turns to a sort of sacred hallucination in Wilson's hands, and that's the essence of his poetic gift: sacred hallucination and vision when friends, family, landscape, ceremony, and living are concerned. In that way, we see why Wilson studied and admired masters like Charles Olson, Robert Creeley and Denise Levertov. Olson, who continually grasped for both the known and unknown in the spirit world, and Levertov, with her conversion to Catholicism, both offered the world a vision of the sublime light, mixed with the cautionary blues of the poet's often dark journey.

In another early poem, "Mantrim," one is never sure if we're here or there, in this world or the world of the spirit. We're certainly, though, in a space also occupied by the deep images of

Creeley and George Oppen, the master American poet who won
the Pulitzer Prize. Here's the poem in its entirety:

> Walk
> -ing
>
> beside
> me
>
> his face
> a high shining
> never
> lost
>
> singing
> &
> the sun
> splits
>
> before
> my eyes
>
> rocks run
> like water

Those rocks, vistas and mesas never disappear in Wilson's
work and serve as totems, in a sense, for spirits to walk on or
through. In his poem "The Celt in Me," Wilson digs deep into his
own blood and taps into the countless generations who sacrificed
and battled others and themselves for a simple step up in society,
only to return to dust once again and the very real specter of
anonymity and a dead facelessness:

> In a museum here I saw a Celtic swordblade,
> Rusted, bent in combat. No handle.
> These men who built what now are shadowed ruins…

And, once again, they don't leave Wilson alone as they haunt his language and almost call him home. Later in the same poem, we learn that the spirit world is, indeed, calling to him:

> From ancient barrows, dim men with old robes
> Walk gravely through the Danube mists
> Their arms outstretched for me.

If the muses for Wilson are rooted in the land and air, they also permeate his work at sea, which is the setting for *Graves Registry*, a book of his days and years spent with the U.S. Navy where he served during the Korean War. Most anyone who has spent time in the desert Southwest knows its connection or can feel the presence of the sea. On many occasions on hikes around West Texas and Southern New Mexico, I've picked up shells in the desert, and it always serves as a reminder that the great vistas were first seas and oceans. And much like the desert, Wilson captures the spirit essence of the sea as its forbearers reach out for him. This occurs masterfully in the poem "SeaDream": *"dark waves, foam/colored to froth/bones, bones/ride darkgreen crests."*

In "StarChart," also from *Graves Registry*, Wilson is secure in knowing that the waves and oceans will deliver the words for a continuing shamanic journey: *"—still I know some starship/will arrive, burst casually forth/with poems."*

Still, time and time again, Wilson returns to the desert Southwest, that place where he both started and ended as a poet. In a sense, we know that his work will go on just as his beloved New Mexico will go on.

In "The Voices of my Deserts," Wilson channels the land and its inhabitants and realizes that all of it, every bit of it, will one day be blown away: the words, the poetry, the homes, the tales, the people, the money. The reader learns, as he or she does through all 1,100 pages, that that's perfectly OK with him. In fact, he tells us: Let spirit have it all, for every bit of mortality needs to be sacrificed for a chance at some immortality that only the desert can understand:

The ghosts of wolves ring our hills.
Those birdcries, Comanche songs drifting
Up from wartrails; the click of steel
In the night, prospectors or old soldiers
sharpening the edge of darkness to a keen
wind that blows all the stories away.

In the end, Wilson is contented with the blowing, rattling, sharpening, crying and howling, for isn't that what great poetry is all about: that channeling of the muses and spirits that deliver the words and worlds? That place of depth and total surrender to the poet's life?

Finally, I have returned to Las Cruces a few times since Wilson's death, but it's always a challenging journey because I feel his spirit everywhere, and I remember his friendship and mentorship and, in a sense, the city passed away for me when Wilson died. Somehow, though, I know he wouldn't want it that way. Perhaps he's whispering right now for me to get back there, to rekindle the friendships, to make a go of it.

Perhaps that journey has already started. But even if it hasn't, there's always the work to return to, those poems and images that keep Southern New Mexico and Las Cruces alive long after the master has gone. In his 1971 poem, "The Old Man Builds a Fire," Wilson stakes his claim for remembrance, and it's a task that we must support, that we should perpetuate by keeping his work alive, first and foremost by carefully remembering his timeless words that remain rooted in his beloved New Mexico:

The geography his hands
leave in the blue air of the shack
are maps, charts of land and trails
the shadowed moccasins of his dreams
have made

New Mexico poems, from **Shaman of the Desert**

Homestead: Carpenter's House

—Fort Sumner, New Mexico

a green frame house trimmed in
white, falling down.

a memory of icetea
served frosted in tall glasses,
of coaloillamps yellow through
old glass windows

—crickets wind
in the cedars, New
Mexico in the '30s
where people lived
for evening & our
old men sat smoking an
hour away

—the darkness, Billy the Kid's
ghost walking
the long road from Pete
Maxwell's house to the Military
Cemetery, alone,
his slender gun with the
birdshead grip
his effeminate laugh
... the shadows.

Old Spanish people who
knew him, stayed off the
road at night, told
these stories of a destroyed
world while all fell down

around them.
small town. a happiness
for children in old stories,
dreaming guns & battles,
bullets that never hurt,
scalpings that somehow
left the hair Intact.

homestead. its uncured wood
rotted in the earth until at last
it broke of its own weight, split
exposing the stained years of the living.

Birdey Riley & Brother: Rustlers

–Out riding

The two, jogging along at dusk.
30/30s stuck into saddle boots,
their horses rested, fed lightly.

They headed up the long draw,
rimrocks faint blue, wind blowing
in harsh, gusting, shifting North.

Above them, the clouds spread
thickened. They put on their slickers,
thunder popped, rolled.

Soon they reached Jesús Montoya's fence,
continued, followed the cow trail, topping
out & there were Montoya's horses, huddled
to the storm. Birdey & his brother pushed
the stolen horses slowly back into the draw
kicking their own mounts down the stone trail.
–a flash, a bolt of light no bigger
than a fencepost hit Birdeys brother
on top of the head, burned through him,
the horse & left wet grass smoking. Birdey
shifted in the saddle, watched the rain put
out the smoldering fires in his brother's clothes,
his hair, then slowly he rode back to town letting
the horses go, to run freely out their panic
while he, solemn, tight faced, went to tell
the undertaker where to find his brother.
He paid the man, rode off, not even changing
his clothes. Later he wrote for some gear.

He was a Baptist preacher by then, called
himself "Richard." This all happened,
1909, Territory of New Mexico.

Trio: Billy-The-Kid

what does it now matter, his name?

a song, one of those bloody marching
chants of the Middle Ages

-a child's nursery rhyme
of destruction & love

children singing:
billy, billy, billy

little girls skipping rope
to gunflashes, boys clutching their
chests, falling to later rise, eat
their suppers & go sweetly to
bed, complete resurrection

billy, billy

Bonney (Antrim-McCarty), Bowdre, and O'Tolliard
rode down the sandy streets of one-horse Mexican towns,
across gullies, their slickers flapping in the rain & wind

   took bright coins for their gunflashes
paid for cattle the same way, spooked them up draws
and sold them wherever they could, for almost nothing

They had a system and their system was luck,
the goddess of the very young, the brave,
and the sick of mind. They rode past *cantina* doorways
hollowing the night with flickering lamps, past general stores

   (remembering perhaps the one
where McSween burned to death and the Kid fled through the
  darkness. firing easily at any shadow?)

64

Past women, girls singing their soft songs, brushing
bare arms against adobe, waiting. The Kid had girls
everywhere, rode on, his silver conchos bright
hand always near his gunbutt

> *Colt* 38 *Lightning* model
> his gun, an undependable weapon with a
> tricky, easily snapped sear. if the sear
> broke, the gun jammed. when it worked,
> the shots lived up to its name, fast as he
> could pull the trigger, a murder weapon,
> not designed for distance shooting, a belly
> gun, for shooting bellies–or backs.

Swept on, the three of them, rustling cattle, stealing what wasn't
    nailed
down, whooping it up, dashing into small towns, their guns
    flaming out
the night, shouting like boys at a picnic ...

He laughed at jails, threw easy smiles & they all report that.
    Charming.
Of course the two lawmen he shot down from behind a wall
    weren't
around to testify, nor were the six Indians he killed while they
    slept in
their blankets. The Colt had its uses.

> *billy, billy*

A handsome young man, with strange colorless eyes,
a good smile and hands delicate as a girl's.
Quick and well-trained, ballet dancer of the Colt,
the rope, the dancefloor

> *billy goat, ram's head his sex on his*

65

saddle seat & tied to his hip

billy

In Old Fort Sumner he had a friend,
Pete Maxwell
      (though it was said Pete was simply
      afraid of him, of his habit of firing from the dark,
      his long memory for wrongs, other people's of course)

He had a friend, and two more to ride beside him
and shout to the clear New Mexico morning.
He had a girl. later to be seen in the street
so fat she had to be moved with a wagon
but pretty then. He had money and fame
and fear, which for him was greater
than any of the others. & such fast hands

he killed Joe Grant with those
      tricky fingers, shifted the cylinder
      of Grant's single-action so that the hammer
      would fall on the empty chamber used
      as a safety, knowing Joe would try
      to kill him. Joe did try and witnesses
      said Joe looked very surprised when the Kid
      slowly & methodically shot him down
            a legend for you, billy
            some dreams that rise
            out of the blood's singing,
            needs that come with the
            bones,
      no-name, no-name
            ya, ya
            he's got no
            nay-ame!
            the children play one
            & cock their capguns

at shadows, hide in
their shallow cool caves
pretending
outlaw lairs
& posses

Pat Garrett trapped the Kid at Stinking Springs,
surrounded the cabin with his men, fired until
they killed O'Polliard. Bowdre, gunned down later
as he and the Kid rode into Fort Sumner.
The Kid turned his horse, rode away fast,
leaving his last buddy in the dust.

They got him later, of course, Everyone knows
that–how he walked in from his sweetheart's shack,
went onto Pete Maxwell's porch to cut a piece
of fresh meat from the beef hanging there to cure.

He heard voices, paused, knife in hand, asked
"Ouien es?" & Pat Garrett, hidden behind
Pete Maxwell's bed, fired at the shadowed youth
filling the doorway. He fell.

In the shocked quiet, Garrett said, "Is it
him?" & waited. Finally the Mexicans gathered
around, turned the body over. *"Si, Senor. Es*
El Chivato." And then the speaker cried, for the Kid
was good to them, did not kill them, and let them feel
he was like them, though he was not, and they knew it.
He was powerful though, and while he himself was a Gringo,
he spoke good Spanish, and he killed Gringos. They loved him,
let him take their women and their homes and their
hearts and still in that Valley it is hard to find
anyone to speak a bad word in Spanish about *El Chivato,*
the little goat who they say was not buried in that
abandoned military cemetery at all but who rode on
& now walks the road by moonlight waiting for his people

to call him, *El Chivato*, the kid with the tricky,
tricky hands, the colorless eyes

O, billy

riding your
thousand horses
kissing your
girls, drowning
in the timed
blood of your

hoofbeats, the perfectly flat
prairies.
llano

estacado,

wave
their grasses

children caught to the hereditary madness of spilled blood and a
glory that dries on the hands, echo your name, the quick
        explosions
of years, dust blowing by your grave & up the valley

billy, billy, billy

The Streets of San Miguel

What have I to bring them, in their
stillness?

dark youths lounging
by the one public phone, old ladies
headed for Mass, the soft wind
against their dark dresses.

If I lived here all my life,
spoke Spanish as fluently as I dream I do,
if one of these lovely boys loved one
of my lovely girls and I was elected mayor,
still I'd be a broken Anglo poet
who has, I'm told, strange eyes,
stranger ways–

who must turn
everything to words while they, so alive,
need so few to speak their loves.

The dusty street, quiet in moonlight,
stretches out ahead. I take a strange walk,
going nowhere. I have nowhere to go.
The ancient houses ring a pathway
to high, windswept mesas.

The Arrival of My Mother

—New Mexico Territory, 1906

She got off, according to her diary,
dressed in a lovely beaded gown, fresh
from Washington with sixteen trunks of ball gowns,
chemises, blouses (4 Middie), shoes and assorted
lingerie. She was at that time about 25, old
for an unmarried woman. Her stiff mother was at
her side, she also wildly overdressed for New Mexico
sun and wind.

What must she have thought, seeing my uncle standing,
hat in hand in the dust of that lonely train house,
cracked yellow paint, faded letters of welcome
for passengers that rarely come?

The buckboard was waiting and they rode out into
the darkness of evening toward the tent, that half
built frame homestead house, wind dying as the sun
sank, birdcries stilled,

I see her now outshooting my father and me, laughing
at our pride and embarrassment. My sister, as good a
shot, waiting her turn. Or that picture of her
on horseback, in Eastern riding clothes beside the Pecos.
A picnic when I was small and how my father lifted me
up
to her and she carefully walked the horse around rock
and sand.

I suppose she finally arrived in New Mexico
in the April of one year when my sister and I sat beside
a rented bed, each holding one of her hands and
watched
her eyes grow childlike, unmasked as a kachina

entering the final kiva of this Dance. The graceful
the slim laughing woman of my childhood. The old
mother
heavy with years slipped away and the woods of New
England dimmed as these dry hills ripened and caught
her last breath, drums, drums should have sounded
for the arrival of my mother.

Twin Aces

back to back, Stud Poker & an open
pot. The play, intense, grew harder.
Clark, Bowers, McMorris & my dad, cool
professionals: "Poker's for men," my dad
say; paying out his debts with grocery money,
bringing his tales with flushed face to our
quiet home. Great stories from the tall
fierce combats he lived for

while I, a comrade,
a spy posted by mother, sat by propping
my eyes open & pleasing father who thought
at last I'd shown a normal interest.

Thick cigar smoke
& the sharp smell of whiskey, I remember
that, & the naked bulb, those men
flicking cards into the pot of light
slitted eyes watching their fall
as if it were their own:

yet my father won
with a slipped ace & we got out quick
before the discards were counted. Walking
home, 4 a.m., my father singing & looking
back over his shoulder, the quiet street
behind him.

–for Richard Russell

Lincoln County War

the high green tall, brightspun
pines, dark earth rich with tales
of the War.

Tunstall, McSween, Brewer,
Bonney

blued guns flaming out
from ambush or siege, hooves
breaking the mountain night, guns

legends of hate, still remembered
as a kind of pride long after
the flashing hands are buried:

growing up, among those
ghosts, their fierce needs
for courage, stiffness

A heritage of murder. The Kid
his queer laugh, high, hysterical.

O'Tolliard, Bowdre who rode beside
him
buried there, with him.

Blazer's Mill where Dick Brewer,
the Kid and some others trapped
Buckshot Roberts, killed him

Roberts shot Brewer, wounded
two others though he
couldn't lift his arms
above his waist, so shot
up was this tough old man

–a legacy fit for
New Mexico, for grim old gunmen,
pistoleros who survived, telling
no stories, their deeds following
them in whispers

walking stiffly down a
street, they were old men,
but the people got out
of their way, their

straight eyes, shiny
Imaginary guns swinging
at their sides:
the glint
of blue, high pines &
gunfire, an empty trail
leading out before them.

–with many memories of John Sinclair

Los Penitentes, *hermanos de la luz*

Hermanos de sangre. Out of a New Mexican night a
memory that
has haunted me all my life
                    penitentes, marching
                    singing, their torches
                    high arc against
                    the crest of the Hill

                    Sensing my mother, her fear
                    I holding her hand, 4, knowing
                    nothing of the needs of men–

                    backs raw from cactus whips
                    yet singing of light, they were
                    truly Brothers of the Light, brown men

                    chanting

                    –little Christs, singing
                    to the agonies, of the wounds
                    of the dying Cristo who led them
                    bearing their sins with his own

                    it is His blood dripping
                    from that sky 64 years ago
                    that calls them forth singing now

                    they, climbing the high Hill
                    with Him, His neck bowed under
                    His cross, they light His way

                    torches, smoking and flaming
                    above the tall grass, after all
                    these years it is the
                    darkness they left behind.

Day of the Snake

My sister, 3 years old in a pinafore sought
shade from our hard New Mexico sun, the white
blazes on the Hereford cattle at the line
camp, her under the one tree, beside the wind
mill

& a rock, beside her foot, out of
shade, grew into awareness,
a prickle at the back of ...
hesitation

the moving coils
dark tongue flicked
out, back

an inch from her foot the rockflat head
steady eyes, her bare foot, vulnerability
of a baby before the sun

& how our father protested
when the rancher killed the heatpassive snake
–a five foot Diamondback–he saying,
with perfect truth, he spared
my daughter, god damn it let
him live

Later, the snake's head crushed, spreading
to rock, rattles quivering musically
we walked
away, blazing suns
about our heads.

Poems on war and peace, and the Korean War,
from **Graves Registry**

LXXIV
Corsair

–to D.S.

It was of course Don
who died.

Blue, with white letters
                    inverted gull
          P&W engine

At full roar, one by
one they returned.

Minus him.

It was of course of course
my friend

                    in the twisted aluminum
                    the shining spars
                    crumpled wheels

                    rudder torn off
                    white letter "V"

splattered with
rice paddy mud

It was of course he
who refused, who would not
kill, would not obey, would
not return–refused

to machinegun civilians
on the Korean hillside
to bomb a courtyard

full of refugees

It was I on the bridge
of the carrier, waiting
counting the planes–marked
the return of the squadron leader,
he who taught him that

> low, slow turn
> just above stalling speed
> the fighter's controls mush
> there, aces away from a spin

He spun. He lay
there and I of course
wait, wait for whatever
second coming there can be
for a splattered flyer
my friend, lying there

who would not kill idly
who did not have the dangerous look
who should've should've fired

–Arjuna, it is not your friends
> you kill but only the shadows
> hiding their selves, Arjuna
> whose spear also rusted in the
> sun

> jagged metal
> the blue, Navy
> blue and a crashed corsair fighter
> over 40 years old and most probably
> no longer there

> a white "V"

to mark another strange victory

78

XXI
Hiroshima

hiroshima. hiro-
shima. hi-ro-shi-ma.

I, an American, try
to say that word, to
pronounce it like
my Japanese girl, turning
my tongue on it
as its own streets
turned & twisted,
radiating outward

–to speak, through
this sign, what
it is to be american,
japanese in a century
of terror

  my face it
shapes itself to tongue;
her eyes gleam back, mirrored,
I speak the word & see
–oval eyes, a burned cheek,
trace the scars
with shaking fingers

How to Sit Here at This Desk Smiling

–Kent State

How long can I continue to act
a part of this country?

        This country.
This beloved land, its slashing
storms and great upthrust mountains,
meadows green and brown, bright under
the clear, sharp sun.

This country where my red brothers
were slaughtered–their gods call
their names from every hill–
where my black brothers, enslaved,
dying scream their pain from cities
darkened and grey with the ruin
of mountains

        & any protest against
a destruction, so clearly seen, gets met
with bayonets, with mace, with clubs
rising and falling, blooded to their tips

How to sit here at this desk, smiling
nodding my head when my fists are clenched
on its polished wood and I give, by my
presence, credence to Their crushing
smashing hatred of this land, of all
that is growing or green

        young and beautiful?

Flowers germinate, raise their blunt
stalks to find concrete sealing them
from the sun; babies cough out their
lives and we wash & wash & wash & wash

How to sit here at this desk smiling?

80

The Poem Politic 3

What are politics anyway
but the formalized lusts and greeds of men?

Dancing figures around a straining body,
the knife is raised high, glints in candle
light the blood is purple, stuff of Kings,
with one high scream the manthing dies
for religion or fun or policy or nothing
at all that any reasonable man can explain.

The Poem Politic 7

These as days, pass, keep
their place, nodding, let us
sleep who would never awake

soldiers! We are all soldiers
(in the sense that we are victim
to wars: our lives themselves, killer

              -moving onward the Christian
banner ahead, gutted children behind
smoke, gas bayonet landmines

beyond one horizon, or another,
the quick sails of warships
gunmuzzles glinting in moonlight

shadows across graves
broken lances, arrows
the shock of cannon
still haunting valleys

Where in America
can you go
that a battle has not been fought
men killed?

in the night
lynched men hang in their trees

leaves ripple
with summer winds
the past, so rapidly
becoming the future,
old graves to welcome
the wanderer

Where in America
can you go?

82

LXII
The Poem Politic 10:
A Note for Future Historians

When writing of us, state
as your first premise
THEY VALUED WAR MORE THAN ANYTHING
You will never understand us
otherwise, say that we

cherished war

> over peace and comfort
> over feeding the poor
> over our own health
> over love, even the act of it
> over religion, all of them, except
> perhaps certain forms of Buddhism

that we never failed to pass bills of war
through our legislatures, using the pressures
of imminent invasion or disaster (potential)
abroad as absolution for not spending moneys
on projects which might make us happy or even
save us from clear and evident crises at home

Write of us that we spent millions educating
the best of our youth and then slaughtered them
capturing some hill or swamp of no value and
bragged for several months about how well they died
following orders that were admittedly stupid, ill-conceived

Explain how the military virtues, best practiced
by robots, are most valued by us. You will never come
to understand us unless you realize, from the first,
that we love killing and kill our own youth, our own great
men FIRST. Enemies can be forgiven, their broken bodies
mourned over, but our own are rarely spoken of except in

political speeches when we "honor" the dead and encourage
the living young to follow their example and be gloriously
dead also

NOTE: Almost all religious training, in all our countries,
dedicates itself to preparing the people for war.
Catholic chaplains rage against "peaceniks," forgetting
Christ's title in the Church is Prince of Peace;
Baptists shout of the ungodly and the necessity of
ritual holy wars while preaching of the Ten Commandments
each Sunday; Mohammedans, Shintoists look forward
to days of bloody retribution while Jews march
across the sands of Palestine deserts, Rabbis
urging them on . . . .

THEY VALUED WAR MORE THAN ANYTHING

Will expose our children, our homes to murder and
devastation on the chance that we can murder or devastate
FIRST and thus gain honor. No scientist is respected whose
inventions help mankind, for its own sake, but only when
those discoveries also help to destroy, or to heal soldiers,
that they may destroy other men and living things

                                          Be aware that
Destiny has caught us up, our choices made
subtly over the ages have spun a web about us:
It is unlikely we will escape, having geared
everything in our societies toward war and combat.
It is probably too late for us to survive
in anything like our present form.

THEY VALUED WAR MORE THAN ANYTHING

If you build us monuments let them all
say that, as warning, as a poison label
on a bottle, that you may not ever
repeat our follies, feel our griefs.

LXXVIII
Somewhere in Washington, in Rome

Somewhere in Washington, in Rome,
the War Office in Bucharest, in Sofia,
Moscow

        –in the great cities of Europe
and America, there is The Book.
I have always imagined it black
calves' leather with heavy gold letters:

    GRAVES REGISTRY

(By now of course each book is fat
swollen with its names and places.
Gigantic, the one in Washington
would bulge the largest room, still
growing hourly with the dead and lost
of the country. Their names, insofar
as each could be identified. Next
of Kin, if any. The nature of the death,
when known.)

Murdered civilians and the enemy–
are not there. Only those who died
in battle or later, in their beds,
their brains burning to the old gunfire
as they faced their last edged night.
He dies, his name appears instantly
within The Book comes a whirring a click
and ink blossoms on the appropriate page.
The Book then waits.

Keith Wilson Bibliography: Major Works

The most complete source for Wilson's poetry is his complete poetic works, *Shaman of the Desert*, published in Livingston, Mt. by Clark City Press, 2009, 1104 pages, paperback. Wilson's work was nominated for the National Book Award in Poetry and the Lamont Prize. The poems from *The Stone Roses* were an outgrowth of his Fulbright Professorship in Romania. His work was also published in innumerable journals.

1) *Sketches for a New Mexico Hill Town* (Wine Press; first edition, 1965; second, 1967).
2) *Old Car & Other Black Poems* (Grande Ronde Press, 1967).
3) *Graves Registry & Other Poems* (Grove Press, 1969).
4) *Homestead* (Kayak Press, 1969).
5) *Rocks, Some Stanzas for Tomorrow-or Yesterday* (Road Runner Press, 1971).
6) *The Shadow of our Bones* (Trask House Press, 1971).
7) *The Old Man & Others-Some Faces for America* (New Mexico State University, 1971).
8) *Psalms for Various Voices* (Tolar Creek Press, 1969).
9) *While Dancing Feet Shatter the Earth* (Utah State University Press, 1978)
10) *The Streets of San Miguel* (Maguey Press, 1977).
11) *The Stone Roses, Poems from Transylvania* (Utah State University Press, 1983).
12) *Graves Registry* (Clark City Press, 1992).
13) *Midwatch* (Sumac Press, 1979).
14) *Etudes* (Limberlost Press, 1996).
15) *Bosque Redondo: The Encircled Grove, New & Selected Poems* (Pennywhistle Press, 2000).
16) *Transcendental Studies* (Chax Press, 2003).
17) *Night & its Secret Songs* (Limberlost Press, 2004).
18) *Fragments of a Forgotten War, a Memorial of Korea, 1950-53* (included in the complete poetic works, *Shaman of the Desert*, as a first time publication, 2009).
19) *Lion's Gate: Selected Poems, 1965-86* (Cinco Puntos Press, 1998).

photo from along old Route 66 by Karen Koshgarian

Gary Worth Moody

End of Water: The Body Recalled *

Dorothy Day, November 29, 1980
the eve of her death

A scythe in air thick with raptors

It is not acrid scent of candle's shiver against rain damaged
ceiling that wakes you.

It is the fluid's frigid

fist around your lungs and heart, as you curl through
sickness's stench into the unborn

shape, a comma in the pesthouse sheets.

Beyond this last fevered bed, you seek a different warmth, a
balm against scabbed

November chill

leaching its way through the Maryhouse brick, etched by acid-
rain. You'd rather a San Joaquin

morning's rapture. The way it lifts

a body toward the sun's skin while mirage heat corrugates
upturned grape leaves.

This is the light you remember.

The farm-workers' strike. A shotgun shimmering in the
grower's gunbull's hands, barrel blue

as Burgundy fruit rotting on

scab-tended vines in rain-starved air while fossilized shells
dissolve to granules of pitted white

working their way inside

your hard shoes, blistering loose the water beneath the skin of
your feet, black stockinged,

88

to match the black dress

you wear forever in the black and white photograph, hands
	clasped upon your right

knee crossed over the left,

seated between two cops, standing with holstered guns and
	riot clubs dangling

from their hips,

before they arrest and transport you to the oven of the desert
	valley's sweltering cells.

The priest has been called,

yet your swollen tongue wants not wafer or wine. A buttered
	tortilla, and common

tin cup you shared

with the striking San Joaquin workers is what you crave. One
	sip, lifted to your

lips from the ditch that quenched

the strikers' thirst under the workers' banner, Mexican eagle
	in flight against red sun

beneath a child angel

lifting the Black Madonna, radiant on the horned crescent
	moon, a scythe in air thick

with raptors, the red-tail's

cry across the vineyards, an antelope squirrel's trill, devoured
	while still alive, and at night,

peacock voices on the drying shed's peaks

mourning the slow sleep of an unperceiving earth witnessed
	beneath the turned black bowl of

ravenous stars.

Scent of dandelion washed into wine

In heat memory's corona, you recall suffrage banners,
    decades ago, damson

and gold, carried

through a Washington mob. Rocks and slurs from men's
    mouths. The nerve

in your left wrist, electric, as

you manacled yourself to the Whitehouse gate. The welt left
    by the policemen's tool when

he pinched away the chains.

The judge sentencing you to the workhouse farm. Being
    herded like a cow to the jailhouse van,

walls tight as a breeding chute,

doors gaped wide as a hearse's mouth. The prison train's
    run across the Potomac trestle

through farmlit dusk to the workhouse

on the Occoquan's edge. Yellow veined bruise on the prisoner's
    cheek after the riot. Momentary

morning sunlight's throw

on the jail's ceiling. Far off squealing of pigs at their morning
    meal after the cell's

unstarred dark,

dank as a grave, flooded with November rain under maples'
    crimson. The shared

straw mattress sanctuary

when they unfastened your cellmate from the bars. The fever
    coming for you when

hunger's ninth night thrummed

your gut for sake of the unsacred vote you never used,
      barely different from the volcanic

heat that almost killed you

when you chose to carve the liquid, beating heart of something
      almost alive

out of your body for love.

Yet now so close to an unwritten end, you long for a shell's
      hollowed shape of caught rain,

scent memory of your broken

water, almond blossoms, and your body's recognition beyond
      sleep, of a different thirst,

the pull of the other's

mouth upon your teat as you watched heat lightning grace
      squall line skullcaps

across Gravesend Bay.

This other, for whom you would abandon life, for whom
      you would breathe,

even beneath the wave.

You remember the way your body lifted itself from small surf
      to music of Russian

gypsy voices, dancing naked,

unashamed, your breasts, pendulous, full with milk weight,
      like those of *La Virgen*

de la Leche, when you gathered

dandelion to wash into wine, now as withered as the solitary
      leaf on the elm about

to be taken by November's unforgiving wind.

Flame, and outside the glass, birds

You pray against the burn that takes you now, as you prayed
     for rain to fall,

where no rain fell, to wash

away the immolant suicide of Roger La Porte, a prayer against
     napalm, a November morning

in the plaza of the United

Nations, beneath water-birds working the air between rivers,
     uplift of pigeons, startled

by the blaze, feathers

iridescent as the gasoline's flare reflected off the library's
     glass, flames so hot

the whole electrical

seaboard grid blacked out that night, darkened cities and
     roads, leaving only marrow

from bones of stars to light

drought stricken towns, as the Catholic worker clung to life
     in an unpowered hospital,

alive the whole

next day, his body's char a sacrifice *against war, all wars*, until
     his breath succumbed

to witnessed fire,

the candle you lit, its heat like some warm hovering just
     beyond the fevered illusory chill,

or the priest holding the uncraved wafer

to your lips. It is not unleavened flesh of God, made man, you
     desire, rather you'd be

as Magdalene, cloistered

in poverty and prayer, at the fringe of metropolis, the true
     wilderness, fed only

by gifts of ravens.

The empty tin cup on the table beneath your leaking window,
    holds water not enough

to quell your body's

waking flames, nor the priest's voice chill enough, to salve each
    ache. Yet, when you dream,

you dream you lie clasped

in some final sensual embrace, nostrils turned toward winter's
    clear air, eyes, unseeing,

yet able to see freezing

rain beyond this cadaverred light, hear, the changed sleet sound
    against glass

until the finch's black beak

plucks the first white flake from vanishing grey. Will it,
    in that instant, be enough,

to remember the unslaked

thirst and tongue's intimate knowledge of everything
    holy and human?

---

* "End of Water: The Body Recalled": This three part poem draws on events described in *All the Way To Heaven: The Selected Letters of Dorothy Day* (Robert Ellsberg, Editor; Image Books, Crown Publishing, Random House, New York, 2010) and Day's autobiography, *The Long Loneliness*. Roger La Porte, a young member of The Catholic Worker movement, founded by Day and Peter Maurin, immolated himself on November 10, 1965, which was also the day of the massive northeast coast blackout that created havoc in the United States and Canada. A professed anarchist, Day's last arrest came at the age of 75 during the United Farm Workers strike in the San Joaquin Valley, for which she served ten days in jail. *La Virgin de Guadalupe* is portrayed on the farm workers' union banner of the time. Though a committed suffragist, Day never voted. She was endorsed for Sainthood by the Catholic Bishops in 2012.

Christine Eber

Waiting for something to fall

Under their sheer weight
murder statistics bury my love for the city,
keep me from going there.
When I think of Juárez I picture
bodies hanging from bridges,
piles of severed heads.

Then a friend, Siba, tells me how easy it is
to cross the border at Santa Teresa,
that I can park my car on the U.S. side
and she'll drive me across.
Siba is a woman who doesn't let fear
stand in her way,
who goes where she is needed.

The officials wave us through
when we swear we aren't carrying any guns
or more than ten thousand in cash.

An asphalt conveyor belt shuttles
workers between factories and homes.
We take it through the desert
from the border to the city.
No traffic today.
The desert is quiet.

Soon the pavement gives way
to the main street of Anapra,
a rutted dirt road dotted with
clumps of people buying and selling.
Vendors stay fluid to evade the extortionists.

A side street takes us to Sofia's house,
perched on the side of a hill,
a gateway into a neighborhood of women

who check in on one another daily,
care for each others' children,
grieve with a family whose daughters' bones
the desert just revealed,
turn old t-shirts into brightly colored flags
that hasten their prayers to heaven.

Sofia beckons us into her yard,
shows me where the prayer flags are made,
offers me a chair and a coke.

We sit and talk about the youth,
how they fear the police,
wish someone would care what they think,
and about the women with cancer,
who will certainly die.

We carry our talk to the kitchen
where Sofia ladles vegetable soup into bowls
and places them on the counter
along with tortillas and rice with peas.

I settle onto a high stool in front of my bowl.
Sofia's dog circles under my dangling feet,
waiting for something to fall.

Nothing pressing calls me away,
no other companions I need.
I come home to the world
that winter day in Juárez.

photo from along old Route 66 by Karen Koshgarian

A Feminist Anthology – Part II

edited and introduction by Dale Harris

Harris

Welcome to Part II of *Malpais Review's* Feminist Anthology. Our Summer 2014 issue presented Part I which consisted of 47 feminist themed poems from 16 women poets: Dorothy Alexander, H. Marie Aragon, Tani Arness, Xochitl-Julisa Bermejo, Joanne Bodin, Debbi Brody, Julie Chappell, Janet Eigner, Morgan Farley, Renny Golden, Veronica Golos, Dale Harris, Kat Heatherington, Pamela Adams Hirst, Michelle Holland, and Ann Hunkins.

In this current issue of *Malpais Review*, Autumn 2014, we complete our Feminist Anthology feature with Part II, 71 poems from 24 poets: Gayle Lauradunn, Maria L. Leyba, Carol Lewis, Lou Liberty, Jane Lipman, Jessica Helen Lopez, Suzanne Lummis, Mary McGinnis, Paula Miller, Judy K. Mosher, Sharon Niederman, Elizabeth O'Brien, Mary Oishi, Marmika Paskiewicz, Susan Paquet, Sylvia Ramos Cruz, Margaret Randall, Georgia Santa Maria, Elaine Schwartz, Jasmine Sena y Cuffee, Marilyn Stablein, Cynthia West, Holly Wilson, and Tanaya Winder.

Bravo, Ladies, take a much-deserved bow! Although there was no effort to be demographically inclusive, these poets are a diverse sample of age, occupation, ethnicity, and sexual orientation. Most but not all are from the Southwest region of the U.S. Many have been previously published in *Malpais Review* but a few are new to our pages. Nor did we try to represent all aspects of women's issues. However, the range of poetic subjects is "Right On!" as I fondly remember shouting at political actions and N.O.W. meetings when a speaker hit a true chord.

To reiterate, the original impetus for this feature was an April 14, 2014 National Organization for Women poetry reading in Albuquerque honoring Sexual Assault Awareness Month (SAAM). It was a powerful event. *Malpais Review* editor Gary Brower suggested I invite those poets to contribute to a *MR* feminist mini-anthology and the list expanded from there.

As a 1960's-70's era activist, I was glad to see a new generation continue the work of raising consciousness. Although there have been great gains towards equality for women, we are far from finished. Job parity, legal status and property rights, safety from domestic violence and rape, access to birth control and abortion, girls' self-image, greater societal respect for women's contributions, all are areas where progress is fragile and in danger of reversal. After all, the Equal Rights Amendment to the U.S. Constitution is still being hard-fought state by state when it should have passed easily decades ago. Internationally, the status of women remains deplorable. News reports are abundant with honor killings, attacks, mass abductions of young women who seek an education, even a recent execution in Iran of a woman for killing a man who sexually assaulted her. There remains much to do.

Poets have ever been the voice for change, and certainly these *Malpais Review* Feminist Anthology poets continue that tradition. We hope you will enjoy the poems and be inspired as you read on!

Gayle Lauradunn

A woman must write her body.

–Virginia Woolf

Here I stand
in this circle of light
feet firm upon
the ground. Plump arms rest
easily. A breeze stirs
long hair. This is
how I stand.

I stand here
in the curves of my body,
my body teaches me
of birth, of love, of death.
My body speaks to me
through the texture
of skin.

Now I stand
in this circle of light
with a child, a sword,
a pen, a ledger,
a violin, a rose.

Gayle Lauradunn

Prose-Poem to a Sister

It is Spain. It is 1476 in the year of our
Lord. A condemned witch is being prepared for
the stake. She says to a friend, some years
younger than herself: Look, they pile the faggots
high! How they fear us, we who generate the action
of flames. Ah, the crowd gathers. Curiosity
draws them. Death is a cold number and the heat
of this death is strange to them. It is a new kind
of dying which comes once the art of life is learned.
Sister, one last request—for the child—do not lose
sight of him. I know he will be a good person,
creative and giving. I do not demand too much
for you are capable of my request. Your fears
are many: there is no need to fear, but you will learn
that for yourself. See how the crowd grows! Their
shapes form a city in the evening shadows. The chill
air pierces their flesh. Sister, read my journals,
then secure them. Their knowledge is for you alone.
When he is old enough, share them with him. Befriend
him. I know I do not overburden you for you have
a strength and a power you are not yet aware of. Hush!
They come for me. Let it soon be deepest night. I
desire these flames to burn daggers against the blackest
sky. Beware the crowd, for the heat draws them!

Gayle Lauradunn

Telling

Sometimes I think I made it up. Try to convince myself that
  he didn't hurt me
that mother didn't turn on me, didn't yell to a five-year-
  old "how could you let him do that?"
Or the old man didn't exist, or the old man didn't do it.
I remember my lack of fear, the pleasure, telling
  Mother.
He could have been 40 or 70. A deaf mute who must have
  wanted to experience as much of life as possible.
  Being left out of sound.
But no he was just a dirty old man.
I only remembered this experience again after many years
  and now it won't leave me.
That old man's face haunts me. I see it even with my eyes
  closed. I couldn't have made it up.
He was tall and slender, almost thin, and wore khaki work
  shirt and pants with a brown belt, wide leather
with a gold buckle. The shirt had seven buttons down
  the front, tan buttons.
His hands were large, square with thick hair on the fingers.
  His fingers warm and gentle inside my panties.
His face had deep lines, the flesh leathery. His
  thin hair black.
He hurt me. He wasn't gentle. But, no, mother stops him
she stops him just as he reaches under my dress. No, she
  stops him just as he pulls down my panties.
She grabs his arm, jerks it away. Screams at him. He runs
  away. He is back
with his hand between my legs, his fingers digging.
  His fingers inside me and I am laughing.
I am daddy's Baby Doll. I am crying. I am pushing against
  him. I am running.
Every man I meet has a lined face. Every man I bed has hairy

101

fingers.
I laugh, cry, with every man. Mother, where are you? No.
    This scene is all wrong. It is a hot July afternoon.
The old man sits with my baby brother asleep in his lap. I
    am five.
No one else is in the house. The doors and windows open.
    Light is everywhere in my grandparents'
house. He is granddaddy's cousin. He wanders and works
    where he can in his boots,
high topped, laced around the ankles. He is quiet. He grins.
    A Halloween mask. Some teeth
stained with tobacco. Outside, the windmill creaks.
    No. It wasn't a dress.
It was a pinafore with lacy ruffles on the shoulders. A
    blue pinafore with white eyelet trim
and white buttons. I was five. He motioned me to him
    pointed to the baby asleep.
He pulled up my dress, put his hand in my panties.
    No. We were outside,
down the hill in the woods behind the house. I followed
    him out into the wavering heat.
I wanted to know his silence. The baby wasn't there. My
    dress was yellow.
It was my panties that were blue. His belt was drawn tight
    around his waist, his pants gathered.
It was there in the dry grass that he did it. Yes, I'm
    sure.
I'm sure. I was wearing a blue and yellow check sunsuit
    and my panties were white. White.

María L. Leyba

Flashing Signs

I want my hands to dance gracefully
casting pirouettes on street corners
like home girls whose fading silhouettes
still haunt me, once they stood regally
claiming 5th/Roma just like laying stake on
their men in lock-up across the street at BCDC.*

They lived life in a giant fishbowl under
Burque's scrutiny clicking tongues they
never heard, just nimbly flashed signs of
undying love mesmerized by stories flying
out of fingertips painted blood red.

How many times I wanted to ask them
teach me how to paint my stories in the
ravaged wind how to push sadness away
every time I visit my son at BCDC
how to joke / laugh find the perpetual
clown in my heart.

On this cold winter day my fingers are
throbbing wanting to mimic magical fingers
of lost home girls now paper ghosts flapping
in the wind like *papel picado* thinking how
rapidly I'll slice the frigid air setting it on fire
with a mother's undying love.

---

* Bernalillo County Detention Center

María L. Leyba

Las Madrecitas

Keep rising lighting fires in
cold casitas rolling tortillas
ignoring achy joints
they keep rising singing,
"Buenos dias de mi Tata Dios"
an unexplained joy warms
their hearts knowing *familias*
are fed before going to work
madres from Barelas keep rising
wearing colorful bandanas, red lipstick /
ugly white shoes singing to the
bus stop downtown in front of Woolworth
domestic workers soaking up hope / dreams
laced in their *chismes.*

City buses rolling in taking them
to forbidden homes of rich *gringas*
Spanish flowing from their joyful lips
tenderly embracing each other like
hermanas, comadres y vecinas who keep
rising needing each other to begin
their wretched day in their blissful chatter
they are renewed energized can face anything
praying for *jitos* lost in gangs, locked-up in jail,
fighting in Viet Nam some try hard to
hide their bruises or *boracho esposos*
Lita with the curved back has cancer still they
beam with pride for popular beautiful
jitas princesas del barrio teasing the one
with a plain brainy daughter secretly
wishing it was their *jita*
no housekeeping job for her.

As the last one enters the bus their
bright colored bandanas become flags
of peace / hope a sign of solidarity waving
for all of Burque to witness the day
las madres de Barelas rose on fumes of
city buses angels rising breathing salvation singing,
"Buenos dias de mi Tata Dios!"

María L. Leyba

Rucka Dreams

She lies in heap of junk
in a fearsome barrio alley
cradled by the bruised swollen
night dreaming of her threatening
lover / his charming
flashing sword slicing her open
like a ripe watermelon exposing
her lonely desperate heart
she tightens the tourniquet
around her skeletal left arm
her trembling right hand
holds a dirty needle with
her elbows she tries to push
her baby girl away swaddled
in a smelly soiled diaper
clinging firmly to mama's tattered
blue velvet blouse, howling into the
forbidden night a wild hungry baby
craving mama's chi-chi's once filled
with sweet milk now turned
bitter black her precious baby girl
she promised to love forever
never abandon like someone
left her years ago
but tonight is a *chiva* night
ripe for *ruca* dreams
greedily she plunges the dirty
needle into blue-black veins
oblivious to her crying desolate baby
collapses on broken glass / trash
passionately waits for her dark prince / his
tainted promises of
I Love You!

María L. Leyba

Sunday Mornings

Waiting is what I do on
Sunday mornings after making
tortillas, *chili rojo y frijoles*
sit / wait for my phone calls
from my adult children.

My son calls first his weekly
allotted call from prison
we have five minutes amazing
how much you can say
he wants to know about Halloween
how many trick-or-treaters did
I have enough candy
who did I see or recognize
what's up in Barelas?

Last week your sister called from
Hawaii from her balcony she
can see the gorgeous blue ocean
miles of white sand / beautiful
swaying palm trees.

He pauses, chuckles well from my
balcony window I see miles of
gray walls wrapped in razor sharp
barbed wire several yuccas refusing
to sway / brown ugly dirt blowing
wherever.

We both laugh!
I'll call you next Sunday same place
same time.

Carol Lewis

1936

It's the 7th year of the Depression
I'm in the third grade
Tonight dad is at his monthly Legion meeting
Mother sends me to the corner Deli
Ten cents worth of thin-sliced baked ham
Ten cents worth of potato salad
We eat in the kitchen
A bare light bulb hangs from the ceiling
The oilcloth table cover is worn
Bare spots interrupt its daisy design
and white woven glued threads show through.
Summer evenings we stroll down to the shores
        of Lake Michigan
And mother tells me someday our ship will come in
Recites our lineage of governors and generals
One evening on Lake Michigan
Our ship proudly anchors in deep water
Blazing like a sunrise
Music swells from the orchestra on deck
Their white jackets snappy as new sails.
We row out to our ship
Mother wears a silk dress instead of cheap rayon
Father's splendid in a new suit
My cotton dress is transformed into sea-foam taffeta
We climb the ladder to the deck
Everyone turns and welcomes us
Compliments and bouquets
And don't we deserve it
We are *aristos* after all
Our vineyards in the south of France
Have been restored to us with apologies
We are among the select.
A cute boy, my age,
Steps forward with a mountainous dish of ice cream.

Lou Liberty

Truth or Dare for Persephone /
Or the Real Story, Please

Was it a day like today, Persephone,
When you took that fateful step
Over the brink,
Into the cleft?

It is said you were raped away
To the dark
And the depths;
Lured with the enchantment
of a flower,
Then captured.

Or –
did you create a diversion, Persephone,
Cleverly distracting your friends,
Slipping beyond taboo to
The edge and then . . . ?
I think no blossom is that
fascinating.

Time having ripened,
Did you play a new game,
Holding the sun in your right hand
And the moon in your left
On a day like today?

Or did you call a storm, Persephone,
Your long hair whirling wind
And chaos
To cover your tracks,
Hide your escape,
A shield against custody?

Your mother cried after you
In sunlight and rain,
She knew only heartache, infinite loss,
Cursing all for your sake
. . . and hers.

It matters not how you did it.
What matters is that you
Did
Go
Deep
Down
To that final caress;
The touch that is
Neither husband
Nor lover,
Neither mother nor sister,
Nor death.

Was it a day like today, Persephone,
When you embraced
The Riddle
And found yourself?

Lou Liberty

Who Solved The Problem And How

It really was too much!
Demeter sitting there,
lost to her grief,
no longer mourning
Persephone but herself
instead.

It really was too much,
darkness and cold,
all suffering so long,
Demeter
self indulgent,
taking everything
with her into shadow.

So Baubo danced
a crone's dance.

Stripped naked,
her withered tits
hanging down,
her wrinkled flanks
quaking with the beat,
Baubo twirled
shrunken paps
left, then right,
prancing her
hootchie,
parading her
cootchie.

All the while, Baubo
moved her hips,
grinding to the east,

swaying to the west.
bumping to the north,
humping to the south.
And Demeter sat
before this lewdity,
untouched, unseeing.

Baudo strutted,
pelvic thrusting
across the room,
shimmying breasts
in Demeter's face,
bumping and grinding,
stomping primeval
rhythm upon
earth's drum.

Baaaah da daaaah,
da da da daaaah,
Baaah da dah
da dah! dah! dah! dah! . . .

Cocking her leg, pointing,
grinning lecherously,
Baubo "smiled" at
Demeter, her
dark vulva
voluptuous,
wanton.

Bending over,
Baubo "winked",
lifting and closing
her butt cheeks,

111

lasciviously
rotating her hips.

Gyrating,
all taboos broken,
cackling as only a
crone can when
she is happy and
outrageous, Baubo
danced.

Confounded at last,
Demeter's lips
twitched.
She smiled, . . .
twittered, . . .
sniggered. . .
Finally the great
goddess lost it –
all that "smiling"
all that"winking",
all that bumping
all that humping –
it really was too much!

Demeter ripped off her
clothes and joined
The Dance.

Demeter and Baubo
pounded the ground,
"smiled" and "winked"
humped and bumped.

Baubo and Demeter
assaulted the heavens
with raunchy,

lustful cries.

Helios,
hidden in his cave,
gave fear
over to
curiosity.

Timidly peeking
above the mountain,
the Sun
caught sight
of unforgivable
antic behavior and
Helios roared
with laughter.

Awe struck, amazed,
befuddled,
unable to look away,
he stayed and watched,
dazzled by the sight of
that dangerous old woman,
that fecund mother,
humping and bumping,
"smiling" and "winking",
shouting and hollering,
tromping their licentious
rhythms on the hard, cold
ground.

The earth cracked.

Persephone blinked,
awakening to fulfillment.

Lou Liberty

The Little Red Hen

Labor unaided.
If allowed, the harvest
hijacked by others.
All women
know this tale.

(They say we know the
truth, even when
very young, from the
cradle they say. I
say from the womb.)

There once was a Little Red Hen who had to bake bread
for her living.
She was unsure and unskilled
but willing
when faced with the task
and the vastness
of the wheat field, the
longtime challenge.

There were three others with whom she lived.
She asked
and offered.
"Help me harvest this wheat,"
she said, "and I will share
my loaves with you."

"Too busy," came one
reply.

Laughter was
a second.

"You must be
crazy," said a third in
ridicule.

So with great difficulty she harvested the wheat herself.

The Little Red Hen had a mountain of wheat to winnow.
She thought
the others would now help
her for anyone could plainly
see that the task was back
breaking for a single laborer.

"Too busy," came the
answer.

Laughter and scornful glance was
the second reply.

"You must be crazy,"
said a third.

So the Little Red Hen worked long and hard and winnowed
the wheat herself.

When the Little Red Hen finished the winnowing,
she had a multitude of
bushels, enough wheat to
feed many mouths for a
long time.

Surely now, she thought,
as she sat exhausted,
surveying the task before her, –
surely now, she told herself,
hoping against hope, they will see
that aid is essential with

all this wheat to grind, much
more than a single person
can accomplish without harm.

Laughter greeted her request.

"Too busy," came a second
reply.

"You really are crazy,"
said the third.

So the Little Red Hen with firm resolve ground the grain
herself.

The Little Red Hen did not ask help with the baking,
loath to face rejection
and ridicule again. On her
own she made the dough
and kneaded it. She shaped
it into loaves, – plain substantial
ones – fancy, braided ones
seasoned with rosemary or
with sweet currants to tempt
and tease the taste buds.

The Little Red Hen collected the wood and stoked the fire
to the right level. Then she
popped in her hard won loaves
and during the baking rested
at last.

Alluring scents flavored the air, wafting through the house,
and the Little Red Hen's spirit
revived, refreshed by the
perfume of her fruitful work.

"I'll have some," said the first,
hungrily waiting by the oven
door.

Giggling with anticipation
the second ran into the room.

"This is just what I need," said
the third, pushing the other two
aside.

The Little Red Hen unloaded the oven as the three anxiously
waited.

She placed her delicious breads on
their racks to cool. From the
larder she got sweet cream butter and
raspberry jam, sage honey and a jug of cool milk.

All of these she placed on the
table. And then
she laid a single place with fine
china and old silver. She brought
one chair and sat down.

"Are you crazy?" said the
first.

The second only glowered.

The third shouted angrily, "Who
do you think you are?"

Softly the Little Red Hen replied, smiling sadly at the
first.

"I am not crazy –

although at one time I was.
That was when I asked your
help. Crazy is repeating actions that
are impossible to accomplish.
But I learned, and
I stopped asking you – so now,
I am not crazy."

"Do not glower and growl at
me," she said to the second. "I will
no longer be intimidated by
your ridiculing laughter or your
menacing glance, although at
one time they almost broke my
heart. But I learned that you
could not touch my spirit if I did
not allow it, so the place at this
table is mine."

"And as for your question," she
said, holding the third with her
penetrating eyes,

"I
am the one who harvested the wheat.
I
am the one who winnowed it.
I
am the one who ground the flour.
I
am the one who made the dough.
I
am the one who fashioned simple
loaves and seasoned fancy ones.
I
am the one who baked them.

And now I thank you, because
I
am the one who has grown strong.
I know who I am.
I
am the one who will eat the
bread of my labor and
I
will savor it alone since you are
no friends to me."

And she did.

The story is ended as you can tell but this is a fable
after all, and requires a moral tag.
The bumper sticker I saw today
will suffice:
"Behind
every
successful
woman
is
herself."

Jane Lipman

Ballad of an Alpha Male's Daughter

To her long-dead father she speaks:
Father, I am not here.
I married a road.
It took me out of town.

I no longer play in the driveway, struck
as you leave the garage. No longer
freeze in your rages or waste my life
resisting your will.

I'm someone you don't know. I'm the nimble-toed,
doe-eyed girl dancing the cucumber ripple
in the halls of Alley High. Father, I have a fog
at my center. The sun pours in my sleeve.

Father, I ran off with a salesman
of tea tree oil dental picks, but left him
for a vermin exterminator, and left *him* to be
a guitar twanged by hillbillies in Appalachia.

A billionaire shipping magnate
married me at sea. Is that a good enough
nar-cis-sis-tic-ex-ten-sion-of-you?
The life you mapped for me wasn't one I would follow.

Father, I married a boat on a river churning
with loss. O the nights of silent tears.
I'm the out-of-place fifth violinist
in a quartet you'll never hear.

   I turned into a cricket
   swallowed by a bird.
   All night I sing in its belly

the loneliest song you ever heard.

I'm a leaf defiled by an aphid.
I asked asylum from the bees
to unbind from your DNA. I float
above the ocean, rewoven.

Father, I married a bat.
All night we fly
on risen wings, up side down,
toward nectar.

Jane Lipman

Borders/*Fronteras*

She drives past locked gate after locked gate.
Only one entrance is open.

She passes destroyed buildings,
a tree graveyard,
rubble.

She stops at the guard booth of the school.

A man snaps her photo,
demands her driver's license.

She hands it over.

We have to do a background check on you.
Make sure you're not a pedophile or a criminal.

She remembers border guards in Russia,
in Poland,
in the Czech Republic.

She knows not to try, not to joke
around the logic of might,
the rant and cant…

but recalls the humanity
in the face of one Russian border guard.

Consciousness travels faster than light.

So when he asked, *Are you carrying any lethal*
weapons? she replied, *My eyes.*
He laughed. And she laughed.

In that moment, no borders, no nations,
no following orders, no automatic
assumption of guilt, no curtailing

freedoms in the name of safety,
no keeping out or imprisoning in,
no giving up.

Just sweet, crazy, unguarded joy!

Jane Lipman

Mystery School

for Judith Soucek Ritter Leigh

1

Sob of the mourning dove at dawn
Fine rain floats through cherry blossoms
I dress, step into misty East Capitol Street
Flower shadows lie on the garden path
beneath exploding forsythia
moist magnolia

Wind rises—
A blizzard of petals envelops me
To be touched by spirit—
fragile translucent pink orange
wet white petals
Slain by their touch

Cherry wings drift
down twisted black trunks
Birds sing inside the petaled boughs
Cherry trees shed moonlight-
colored blossoms—
swirling around dark bare trees
that haven't yet come to leaf

Cherry lace frames the Capitol
Jefferson and Lincoln Memorials
For a moment Washington remembers
its origin Ornamental cherries fruit cherries
reflect in the Tidal Basin's
petaled water fallen stars
I used to live here It comes over me
how I love this city

There for a workshop on Ancient and Modern
Mystery Schools, Kabbalah and Masonry
held at a Scottish Rite Temple
Lodge of the Nine Muses
where elements of the Constitution were birthed
Back home in New Mexico what stays with me
are the cherry blossoms

2

When she died, my dear friend took off, didn't hang around
for even the obligatory three days
Perhaps the length and ravages of Parkinson's
bardoed her straight to Paradise
I hadn't thought to ask her to send me a sign
from the other side
Twenty-six days after she crossed over—
in meditation with my friend Reita—
I'm ecstatic beneath a cherry tree by the Potomac

Blossoms cocoon me in soft rain
as far as the eye can see—arcing from above
carpeting the ground drifting
Love suffuses everything
I realize Judith is here This is Judith's *baraka*
and dissolve in tears
clasped in her love that blessed my life

A medicine man stopped her once near a pyramid in Mexico
said her aura was vast as the mountains
Yes, and here it is in cherry blossoms
the dew of heaven
enfolding us and the whole Tidal Basin
We're all mixed up with the blossoms
monuments, Masons
even the federal buildings

3

I think of Reita when Z'ev ben Shimon Halevi asked
in the D.C. workshop if there was a Buddha in the room
Reita raised not one but both her hands
mystified by the rest of us who didn't
It comes over me that when cherry blossoms fall
they fall on the ground laughing
like me right now—at how

a woman tells the Kabbalists and Masons
that she's the Buddha
Cherry blossoms, Judith, Reita and I
laugh ourselves straight to enlightenment
The Kabbalists and Masons join in
the universal jamboree
God
beholds
God

Jessica Helen López

Cunt. Bomb.

the c is as insidious
as a paper cut
as pleasurable as a paper boat—
if you happen to know how to fold
one and let it ride

the u of it lies between your legs
look down lovingly
lucky you if you happen to have one

pet it if you will
pet it as if it is the pet
rabbit your mother
never let you have

the cunt is absolutely
not a bomb
it will not hand-grenade explode
your skull open like a cantaloupe

brain matter writhing against
the wall behind your head

it will not shred your hands
to lace if you happen to finger
the trigger every now and now

the cunt *is*
most definitely
a bomb

you may strap it to your chest
and there it will reside like
your own personal rattlesnake

do not attempt to rob banks with it

Do however –

tell your boss that you own a cunt
(you have the receipt to prove it)
and watch how on the inside
he faints like little boy blue

Do however –

tell your teacher that you can spell cunt
that if you happen to extract letters
from the available alphabet
and arrange them in a certain fashion

this is what
you get:

C-U-N-T

the cunt is not a rude house guest
soiling the kitchen towels, sneaking
bacon scraps to your arthritic dog

the cunt is not a rapist
nor a necromancer

because Webster says it so
cunt is the most disparaging word
in the English language

it will make men
both want to fuck you
and bash your face in

because of this they are fire engine
red-faced
and embarrassed

because of this
you should wear it
like a good perfume on
the soft side of the wrists

which is to say the n

forces your tongue to the
top of your mouth
causing you to bare
your teeth ever slightly so

Nnnnn—

note that the t is the marvel of it all
tying everything up
in a neat and tidied corset
like a coin purse

or a straight jacket

Here are some fun things you too
can do with the word cunt –

Google it and it is insured
you will have hours of fun

hold it to the sunlight
like your favorite kaleidoscope

create a word search
in which every word is
the word cunt

reconcile the word cunt
by writing a poem no one
will ever publish

challenge yourself to define
the word cunt to your nine year-old daughter

rack up a triple letter score
next time you scrabble

translate cunt *en espanol*
and impress your folks
with such tonguetastics as –

chucha
choncha

cucha
cuca

and the ever masculine version –

coño

there is nothing
more sensual than
a cunt who can wear a *tilde*
like a party dress

recall that the cunt
yields great power
which is to say
it will scare a great many
people

one last
recommendation

scrawl the word cunt
on one hundred and one
small pieces of white paper
each a small and distinct snowflake

insert into randomly selected books
located on the shelves of your
favorite library

walk away and wait
watch the fallout
for years and years and years
to come

the word cunt
will float
back down to earth
like confetti
or a deafening
ash

Jessica Helen López

What the Womb Isn't

Feminism is a socialist, anti-family, political movement that encourages
women to leave their husbands, kill their children, practice witchcraft,
destroy capitalism and become lesbians.
—Pat Robertson, political sphincter

the womb isn't your cemetery
your fire escape, your sticks
and stones diatribe

it isn't empty swan song or slick-shoed pole dance

it isn't without fire, without magnanimous
thunder roar nor the strength of eggshell around embryo

it is all things physics
it is all things holy and unholy

the womb
the belly
the mound
the convex and concave
the body song
the abortion
the birth
the afterbirth
murmur congealed
purple and pulsating placenta

the womb isn't your political bastard
your 5 o' clock news
top story whore
ballot stuffer
wedge issue appetizer plate

the womb isn't
the womb isn't
the womb isn't
a third-rate quote

it is fire-spark
it is Corn Goddess
Tonatzin, eater
of the good filth
and maker of man
and woman

the water-rush of menses

it is the last blood kernel
protected by the husk

Suzanne Lummis

Letter to My Assailant

On such occasions
one comes to know someone spectacularly fast.
Even with your unfriendly arm at my throat
you could hide nothing from me.
Your failures with women, for instance,
filed through my mind.
And I knew your father was hostile to doors.
He liked to slam them or break them down.
Your mother worked her way up from dimestore
to drugstore. Even in her grave
her hopes kept shrinking.
Now she's thin as a spindle.
I even knew without looking
your socks had red diamonds
like a small town boy's. In fact,
with my breath stopped in my throat
your whole life flashed past my eyes,
but I didn't let on.
"I can't breathe,' I gasped,
and you loosened your hold.
I suppose I should have been grateful,
instead I felt impatient with men,
with their small favors.
I suppose you felt the same about me.
You'd no sooner reached through my torn blouse
when my screams made you bolt.
We leapt from each other
like two hares released from a trap. Oh, oh,
something's not right between men and women.
Perhaps we talked too much,
or did we leave too much unsaid?
When you ripped my shirt mumbling
"I don't want to hurt you,'

I replied, "That's what they all say."

I'll admit I was glib if you'll admit
you were insensitive. Look,
the world is brimming with happy couples,
benign marriages, with men and women
who've adjusted to each other's defects.
Couldn't we adjust to each other's defects?
I'll begin by trying harder not to forget you,
to remember more clearly
your approximate height, your brown shirt
which I described to the police.
Our encounter must stand out in our minds,
distinct from all others.
I never intended
all this to become blurred in my memory,
to confuse you with other men.

Mary McGinnis

You Are Losing What Has Always Belonged To You

Native woman
I see us leaving you

The way you leave yourself
abandoning your strength and solace
dropping your certainty in gravel
thin and lifeless as your mud-caked lips
The shell of yourself in washed-out brown
pulling your emptiness across
the sun's yellow knife

The sharpness of stones is pulling you under
We hear you speak but do not understand your signal
passing you too quickly on our bike
caught up in our own road's meeting

Your syllable stays with me
I will remember you stumbling for the ditch
only your head still visible
Imagine your hands as ragged curtains
over your face closing out the day—
You would go no further
lonely as a woman without ancestors

Writing about you in my varnished house
healthy and white with my allergies and sunburn
I ask which of us
will open herself into death
understanding the wound and blessing of her life

Mary McGinnis

A Hand Embedded With Nails

A long and tapered nail
has pierced her delicate hand—

As you said these words, for once I was glad I did
not see or feel her
dark blood.

Even as I long to drift away, as
my mother once did, saying what will
be will be, you say there's a mirror where
each of us can see our own faces.
I or you could have been pulled into the dark, dragged away,
erased and splintered into bone and white ash.
Did I say I am lucky?—a

woman allowed to create her own self-torture then
I can turn and walk away at will; no need to
tell me how to be
happy and dense with ignorance,

now that the hand has dissolved
along the border between sleep and waking.

Mary McGinnis

Meditation on Chipped China

On the third shelf from the bottom I keep
platters, glass plates,
one single blue plate, shallow soup bowls;
on the fourth shelf: a heavy clay plate,
chipped plates from the Albuquerque flea market,
a bowl with faux gold designs, and two goblets
for drinks yet to be poured,
and those antique plates from her Aunt Lillian that C. gave us—
the aunt thought a girl should go straight from her father's house
to her husband's house. When C. got married,
Aunt Lillian gave her these dishes and said
I'll sell this house for much less
than it's worth—handing her keys to a cage.
She found herself a man with a weak handshake, and no
personality who worked as an accountant by day,
drank and dressed in drag at night,
and began each day with vodka in his coffee.
And after the whirr of wifely duties,
Chinese meals made from scratch,
there were beatings and threats.
Yet those dishes weren't broken when they fought.
When she came to New Mexico and met a new man,
who bought her a Southwest set, she gave her old dishes to us.
Higher up, I keep the demitasse cups
You bought me during a thunder storm
In December 1969.

Paula Miller

Cape Cod Canal

Who told me the Canal tide would turn
after slacking off for twenty minutes
before running off to Boston or New York?
Before I stepped off Pierce Point Rock?
Before I took up the dare to swim across and back?

Treading water in the slack I tried to remember.

As I approached Buoy number 9
its bell bonged twice in response
to a yacht's passing wake,
and set off the roll of waves
that heaved me up and down
until I just let go and rode the swell.

As slack tide passed the 15 minute mark -
in that pause before I made my bid to finish -
I remembered   it was my older brother
who didn't like me anyway
who thought I was a nuisance
who would rather see me swept away
either to Boston or New York.

Paula Miller

Dream Talk

I remember you flush with moonlight,
the round of your face
mimicking the curve of stars
as they taste the space around
Scorpio's sting.

Are you still in the garden of delight
beside moonbeams   entangled in stems
of red hollyhocks   dreaming of being yellow
like roses   purple like asters
fragrant like lilacs?

Today, spring peepers gossip in the cattails,
old bullfrog croaks on his pad -
deep baritone king of the pond.
I see young turtles sunning
on the sodden half-sunk log.

At pond's edge I recall your winsome body
swaying   lilting in cool summer evenings
filled with such deep longing
to move the moon into your arms.

Paula Miller

Faded Calico

I remember the faded calico apron you wore
as you busied yourself making jam   canning peaches,
the click of your false teeth as you said   *elegant,*
the stays of your corset hard beneath my fingers
when I gave you a hug   looked in your wrinkled face
for reassurance after a difficult sibling battle -
the kind that rattled the old farmhouse windows
threatened even the flocked wallpaper on the staircase,
already minus a few spindles from previous rows.

I thanked God for the peace of your pink carpets,
blue velvet rocker with its crocheted doily
well-worn comfort of your flowered easy chair
glass candy jar filled with sour balls and mints,
and most of all for the generous warmth of your big body
withered hands that wiped tears
quieted the pounding in my heart.

Today I visit your grave-site offering red geraniums.
They will fade like your calico apron,
while memories I keep of you remain
bright and vivid in my mind.

Paula Miller

Altamira Afternoons

I loved her name – the way its vowels rolled off my tongue:
Idaida Maria de la Coromoto Arvelo Bustamente.
I loved that she was a Virgin of Mary of the Coromoto.
She lived across the street in the half house
her family shared with Silvia Rodriguez
whose father stood on the porch in a muscle undershirt
to yell and quarrel with the day over his coffee.

I waited for her every afternoon about four
when the blue school bus opened its jaw doors
and her tiny form in its perfectly ironed
navy blue tunic and crisp white blouse
stepped down, hefted a backpack
mountained with books
onto those spare shoulders.

We unbound her pack and examined
the days' lessons, marveling at the cards
of other Marias - of Guadalupe, Avila and Iguerote
all Virgins in high colors and mournful tints.
Idaida showed me the Saints Days on her calendar
introduced me to the delicate gold virgin medallion
she wore nestled behind the agony of her crucifix.

She fetched a folded white towel from her bed
and disappeared into the bathroom for her
afternoon bidet cleansing ritual.
What had the nuns at the Immaculate Heart of Mary
told her about cleanliness and the
proximity of God to those whose "down there"
parts were cleansed of the day's sins before
the ritual rosary hour arrived?

We gather together at 5 o'clock, the sacred hour,
Mama, Abuelita, Tia Maria Ana and Abuelito.
Circled in a small pink terrazzo-floored room
at the very heart of the house
lace curtains filter outside sounds
as we pick up the holy beads,
pluck them, say them, pray them -
we celebrate Maria Madre de Dios

A simple chain of beads, some clear, some opaque
with the tiniest silver latched separation
between each phrase;
each one meant to be singled out
each one greeted with an Ave, Santa or Salve Maria.

I had never heard of God's mother, of Mary, or a Virgin -
any holy woman in God's solemn kingdom;
but, in an instinctive instant –
in a leap of faith and burst of joy
a feminine bud sprouted within me.
I began running with the rosary
with all the Marys, - virgins, mothers, others -
a long marathon over years
of Un beaded meaning.

Judy K Mosher

Comfort Clothes

My ragged, white-cotton, frayed shirt with the
cuff barely attached to the sleeve anymore,
comforted. Soul deep,
even as others disparaged it.

You know the kind, I'm sure you have one, too.

But as I chopped wood,
carried the water of Mother's elder-years,
that shirt grew more threadbare.

What use is there in saving these threads?

Sit here, drink tea, tell me your story,
I'll tell you mine, of the final thread
unraveling forever our last
beloved comfort clothes.

Judy K Mosher

Red Scissors

fragile fingers
squeeze the scissors
papers cut precisely

at eighty-six, her scissors
always park themselves beside
her frayed maroon placemat

she hides things there–
treasures clipped from magazines,
newspapers, even her mail

tidbits for conversation
smother under that placemat
revive when visitors come.

silver blades with red handles
in perfect reach
for moments like this

when the hope of the
winning lottery ticket
falls like spent confetti

scissors then return to their
proper place as CNN
blares today's other bad news.

Sharon Niederman

Class of 2010

Your father's up there, somewhere, in the bleachers
with his new girlfriend, not much older than you
Nervous, tattooed, huddled in the corner
murmuring into her cell phone
she's going out for cigarettes

Last time you saw him
you were eleven, screaming, out of control
Cops came in the middle of the night
After he threw you down the stairs
he put your mother in the hospital

For years you made your own breakfast
got yourself and the others off to school
Booze on her breath, you took care of her too
She's up there crying
You've made her proud

You can't wait to get away
No idea where you're going
Two year Missouri junior college
The counselor handed you
a full ride, your ticket out

Pomp and circumstance
Pomp and circumstance
You march to that bleary rhythm
Step on stage, in long gold robe
wobbling on your four inch heels
This time you will not fall.

Sharon Niederman

I Am No Rapunzel

I am no Rapunzel
Not even close
Yet I climbed the winding staircase
to the castle turret
like that Nordic princess with long flaxen braids
whose destiny declared she remain locked within.

I laid a fire in the grate
Spent my days
wrapped in my velvet cloak
Watched mountains
emerge from clouds
I slept under comforters of down
Woke at dawn to the howls of the pack
unable to remember dreaming
My hair grew longer, down to my shoulders
I studied membrane of feathers, crystals, pine bracts

My falcon returned from his green hill flight
bringing me meat, yet I was not tempted
I strummed themes of solitude along my library shelves
Brewed strong tea to console myself
for all that was lost and could never be
My hair grew down my back, turned silver
The mountains shone gold, gave their harvest of sunlight
and still I had no appetite.

Who among us would willingly reinvent herself
were she not exiled from her dreams
Like Rapunzel, casting long hair over the balcony
praying for the strength to hold.

Sharon Niederman

Is That All There Is?

You were wrong
The purpose of life is not to be happy
You get your moments, of course
You breathe in to remember
breathe out to forget

You were not put here to lay your head in an oven
like Great-Aunt Rose
who tried Christian Science first
You didn't come all this way
like Grandma Goldies
sick for three weeks in steerage
forced to live with her mean uncle
or sent to work in the sweatshop at fourteen
like Grandma Sarah with her Polish blue eyes
You would never be like Aunt Clara
who gave her ring finger to the meat grinder
hung the strap on the kitchen door
Or Aunt Mary, who got pregnant first
Or Aunt Elaine, who put Minnie away

You were not given voice to hum Anna's favorite tune:
"Is that all there is?"
She did the best she could
she told you often enough

You walked the beach collecting shells
hoping for a dolphin sign
You ran down the hillside to the river
of Indians and revolutionaries
You pledged allegiance
recited the Lord's Prayer
Made friends with the French horn player

the new girl from Michigan
the drum majorette, destined for soap opera
the peacemaker who loved to dance
the professor's motherless daughter
Together you bowed your heads
Sang bye bye birdie

You miscalculated badly
but so what?
Smoke snakes from burning ditches
sandhill cranes track this river north
willows glimmer the possibility of green.

Sharon Niederman

Wars Ago

Remember when the sight of a fallen sparrow
broke your heart? You vowed to tell its storyAs if storytelling
would save the broken lost
Remember when you marched down Fifth Avenue
swore to end the war, so many wars ago?

Remember when you came to town, fell in love with
desert sunlight, Indian drums, the discovery itself
Placed a pawned turquoise ring on your finger
Promised you'd never leave, and you haven't

But today you left the museum
walked downtown Central Avenue
Met the toothless beggar in torn black lace
offered her your last dollar bill
 "What for?" she asked,
then looked you in the eye
for the first time.

Sharon Niederman

You Will Know the Time

You know you are getting old when
you trip on a sidewalk crack
Walk head down, afraid to fall again
Ache when you get out of bed
Drive with one arm on the wheel
protecting your injury
You find the medium's vision impossible
Too late now to move to the coast
become an Olympic figure skater
believe your forgiveness has healing power
There is no starting over
You stand at the vegetable counter
debating the merits of baby spinach versus swiss chard
out loud, for all to hear
Your ghosts stroll Central Avenue, coffee cup in hand
Lovers whose love-making you've forgotten
but whose broken children you still carry
The seller of enlightenment recognizes you
You pretend to know him
Perhaps you do, after all.

Elizabeth O'Brien

Ghost Ranch Dawn

I catch a glimpse of her this morning
just before sunrise she climbs the ladder to
the adobe roof bundled in familiar black
headscarf riffling in the wind
she sits in front of a small easel staring South

a raven swoops down lifts her to his wings
on thermals they flap across the flatlands
to mesa top raven pours her into Pedernal
stark lines transfigure into soft mounds
a sleeping woman pulses volcanic energy

the wind rustles she is back in her chair
growing more and more angular
head flattens arms fatten curve down
feet turn tuff white she glows deep gray blue
casting long shadows toward the horizon

still as rock she electrifies the air with her breath
in slow motion she dabs black to blues on the canvas

Do I see lightening pour through her hand or is it just
tuff-white flashing the rhythm of her brush?

Elizabeth O'Brien

Tending Roses

Bessie pours lost dreams into roses—
each spring prunes dried stalks
turns soil around the roots
fertilizes, sprays

in dry springs she runs a black
rubber hose from house to garden
puddling water around each bush
singing—a new mother awaiting birth

as weather warms
she walks up and down rows of roses
in straw hat, carries sharpened hoe,
strokes new leaves as infants

June garden fills with bursting blossoms
bees hum, rain gentle
soft-peach yellow pink greet dawn
white glow under summer moon

her darkened parlor brightens
summer long with crystal vases
American Beauty, shy Peace
filling pockets of loss with rosy scent

Mary Oishi

the reason for poetry?

i do not wish to use my boots to trample death
nor my words to glorify
a young woman at the poetry reading tonight
believes the man who said
the reason for poetry is death
i'd like to take her to a nearby canyon
where waxy yellow and fuchsia flowers
spring from the cacti
see if she can find a poem there
or to the maternity ward to watch a mother
breastfeed her baby for the first time
see if that mother's eyes
may hold a thousand poems
perhaps tired   but far removed from death

i'd like to show that woman
two lovers in the midst of war
but lovers nonetheless
let her hear the poems in their moans
beading on their backs like sweat
i'd like to take her gently by the hand and say
don't take on everything the men say
as Truth for you   even if they're poets
trust your womb   your second heart
see if it does not tell you
the reason for a woman's poetry is
Life

Mary Oishi

women when we rise

women, when we rise we rise heaving
panting, pushing, screaming like
big bang birthing, when we rise
women, when we rise we rise against
pain, through pain, through pain,
through more pain than one body
can stand it seems

women, when we rise it's never just
one resurrection it's always
bringing more life with it,
pulling the whole underworld along
it's bursting tombs into
seedlings and springtime and
singing tomorrows when we rise

women, when we rise truth mountains
shadow-darkened for centuries
burst watermelon and high-lit ribs
plain as day for a hundred miles
when we rise
women, when we rise
secrets cry out from crevices
sulphured springs transform to sparkling,
what once was poison now is fuel
for still more rising when we rise

women, when we rise there is no
wind can take us down
tethered as we are to moon and myst'ry
women, when we rise all else is trifled:
all the foulest deeds of greed and war
all fears that spawn them gone
when women find their power

women, when we rise we rise together
out of bones unnamed and cries forgotten
bonded to our cells like
witch to stake, like slave to chain,
like hiroshima vapor to the stone,
like juarez blood to desert sand
but when we rise we bring them every soul
from the first mother forward
and goddess breath will roar from us forever
when we rise

women, when we rise we must not,
cannot, will not be put down again
when women rise
when women—
women rise!

Susan Paquet

"Aunt Stella"

(Estela Ibarra, September 13, 1913 - July 30, 2011)

Aunt Stella came to me in a dream last night
Invited me to lunch at Leo's Restaurant
I said, "But Tía Estela, you are dead"
The uncles told me you died last year
Tía said, "Never mind, meet me at noon"

She sat at the table, straight and tall as always
We ordered, "tres banderas", tri-colored enchiladas
We laughed and gossiped
Then I grew sad, remembering she was dead
She saw my tears
I told her again, the uncles say you are dead

      She leaned close to me
            Mijita, my child, listen to an old woman
            Never let your reality, be defined by men
            Let's order dessert

Susan Paquet

Dolores

(a modified Sestina)

Dolores never knew why she fell in love
that hot summer day on 4th of July
hot dogs, apple pie and Hawaiian punch
a handsome brown eyed man
longing to lust, to baby on the way
fire works, snap-crackle-pop

Never wore a sun dress after that July
too many bruises, from too many punches
He stroked her hair, saying just his way
of showing strength of his love
Could she ever leave her brown eyed man
as she fed their kids, cereal, snap-crackle-pop

When she told him third baby was on the way
his anger raged fire hotter than July
Dolores understood this was not love
She raised a hand to shield herself from this man
fueling the strength of power behind his punch
Dolores' bones broke, snap-crackle-pop

Dolores knew this would be his last punch.
The air became empty of love and thick with July heat.
Then screamed the snap-crackle-pop of gunfire.

Susan Paquet

Nothing Left but Ninety Four Stitches

Kayla Renee, pretty young thing
  born August 1994
Raped by second step daddy
  year 2004

Kayla Renee birthed two babies
spawned by her mother's men
before she slammed out the door

Life of street hard place to land
Johnny Lee handsome as could be
picked her out, then picked her up
swore he would love her truly
said, just drive the car for me

Parked her outside the bank
kissed her on the cheek
left the motor running
told her gun was just show

She saw him walk inside
then heard, gun fire
He jumped in the car
screaming just drive
car hit a curb, blew a tire

Johnny Lee got away
Left Kayla Renee to take blame
Left her with prison time to pay

Left Kayla Renee with 94 stitches
  as prison medics tore his baby from her body
Pain muffled by concrete infirmary floors

Nothing more is left for Kayla Renee
   A pretty young thing
      born in August 1994
but pain of 94 stitches
silenced behind prison doors

Susan Paquet

Tell Tale Bruises from No Limit Poker Game

Papa played poker for fun and money
best poker player in town
      lucky and smart
studied and understood
world of hundred dollar bills
      billowing in cigar smoked rooms

In grade school
      Papa taught me poker
Sunday afternoons playing for match sticks
Papa taught me strategy
predicting opponent moves by their "tells"
clues as to what their hand held
revealed by eye twitches and voice tone

Before I had even learned to roller skate
      I knew the foreboding clues of mother's
harsh hand crashing against my body
I knew the signs
kitchen smelling of burnt toast
Mother's voice tight as cat about to yowl
jaw clenched as she scrambled eggs
in blood red Pyrex mixing bowl

After the three of us ate breakfast
Papa. oblivious
left for work
leaving me alone with mother
I became her mark
her no limit poker game
her entire hand against me
palms, fists and nails

As a child. I assumed
Papa could only read "tells"
in cigar smoked rooms
that he never saw my bruises
why else would he have left me
all alone with her

Marmika Paskiewicz

It's A Class Thing

the herstory of all
not hitherto existing
except in the shadows
society of giving birth
and cooking breakfast
is the herstory of
laundry   dishes   hiding invisible
becoming visible   opening into currents
of the time
class yes struggle yes fight yes

(once bought a game from ms magazine
with special cards for
paychecks home public life
make it to the statue of liberty in the end)
(a deck of cards with pictures of the grimke
sisters elizabeth sojourner bright eyes)

alice b fired from $2400/year teaching job
in texas panhandle when fbi agents
arrived from washington
fired for signing a paper once joining a party
asking haves to share with have nots
new history not allowed
herstory certainly not

don't go to the spanish club dance with guero
if you want any of the popular girls to
speak to you of course they never did
it was a class thing and she didn't clean her
fingernails either
and her mother a teacher how could she

161

age 4 lilia says i don't know who i like best
susan b anthony or florence nightingale
don't forget emily

constant opposition   reconstitution
first one then the other
ruin   revolution
common   ordinary   everyday
before   forever   after

Marmika Paskiewicz

The places that call us

"Here, see here. We buried your umbilical cord here
in the house so you, our girl child, will nest inside."
                                        –Pat Mora

I never asked my mother
what happened to my placenta –
                        I'm sure it wasn't buried under a
Christmas tree
like Lilia's on Kentucky Avenue –

I'm sure no trace came home
from the hospital with us –
                        everything sterilized, cleansed, disposed
                        in the aftermath of war
                        in the presence of war

She never thought of it twice –
remembering rather the husband not with her
but at the race track
hedging his bets
as he always did for the birth of a child

                        a birth of a daughter a lucky day
                        lucky after two strapping sons
                        lucky after a third boy born dead.

"Nora will be her name,"
said Mother, "because of Ibsen."
"No, Laura," Father overruled,
for his aunt, Minnie's sister.
                        So I became Laura

but Mother won in the end.

Wandering in dusty library stacks later
looking for something else
I found it was Laura,
the woman Ibsen knew –
she the one who left her dollhouse
for a life she could own.

My own placenta probably
thrown into a bucket of hospital waste
or sliced and dissected by medical students.
Later my mother left her own
dowdy dollhouse,
four children holding her hands,
her skirt.

And I've never been drawn to a house in Ohio –
but to hospitals, libraries,
museums, universities

Sylvia Ramos Cruz

A Place of Our Own

We gather in my living room in Riverdale
above the dark still waters of the Hudson
for dinner in a space devoid of men;
a space where we can sit relaxed
free of male clothes and attitudes donned
each time we go into OR, ICU, Emergency;
a space where we can let our guard down
re-arm for the battles of another day.

Spread around the spacious room
eating take-out food (my culinary talents
undeveloped, more lack of interest
than lack of time) the few who inhabit
this man's world are as different
from one another as we are from them.

We are the tough-as-nails woman, the one-who-cries-
the-fattest-tears-ever-seen woman, the flaky woman,
the much-too-soft woman, the maybe-too-old woman,
the pretty plump woman, and I, the one-who's-been-
through-the-whole-process-and-still-stands woman—
so I've heard us called.

Occasionally, my nine-year-old daughter wanders in
drawn by the jokes and laughter, clinical anecdotes,
sobering stories and, yes, ranting-and-ravings of women
who chose to take the knife against all odds.
To her, we're all just fine.

Sylvia Ramos Cruz

Barredor

Wilted tobacco leaves hung from rafters
like spent dirty handkerchiefs. Below them
village women sat on the ground stripping central veins,
plaiting resinous half blades into thick braids
they coiled into rolls that left deft fingers
sticky and stained and Papá Juan tied
to the flanks of his mare, rode to town,
sold to auctioneers on the plaza
across from the church and city hall.

Las mujeres kept careful track
of which pile of withered leaves they used
for each roll so as not to mingle leaves segregated
by quality into three. I never remember
the names of the other two, just the *barredor*.
These were the broad leaves that sat at the bottom
of the stem where they brushed earth
swish-swishing in Caribbean winds,
crawled and munched on by a host of insects dying of DDT,
trampled by children running like escaped prisoners
after school to climb mango trees.

Barredor, floor sweeper, never expecting
to be more than just good enough
to go into cigarettes or chewing tobacco.
No expectation of becoming a Havana
good enough to be clenched between the teeth of Fidel Castro
as he looked defiantly across the sea at JFK.

The women's furrowed faces,
tar-splintered teeth, tobacco tanned-hands
made them look decades older.
They chattered constantly as they weaved,

laughing at stories they'd heard a million times,
spitting thick *tabaco* juice into corners of the barn,
cotton skirts sweeping the dirt floor as they leaned-in
to plunge fingers into aromatic pyramids
they spun into brown gold.

Sylvia Ramos Cruz

Chopped Liver

The pungent slightly metallic smell of Mrs. Weinberg's
chopped liver wafted in the air belched by factory smokestacks
just a few blocks away from the anatomy lab
where Roger Rhatz, Ray Reich and I gingerly picked apart
the greater gluteus fibers bound to Mr. Green's formalin-pickled
sacred bone. It brought memories of mom's cumin-speckled
chicken livers in brown sauce that my sisters and I would eat over
    rice
building our stores of iron against the day the heavy red metal
would flow from our bodies in a ritual of monthly purification
designed to turn us into child-bearing dutiful wives.

I remembered my mother's story.
In the early days of their marriage my father loved her
liver and she loved cooking it for him.
He would arrive famished after a long day lugging
Underwood typewriters riding city buses from one business to
    another.
The rust-colored fleshy delicacies were guaranteed to salve his
    spirit,
if not his feet. When he started college, he took a night job in the
    morgue
at the hospital where my three sisters and I were being born.
One day he came home pea-faced and peaked
and told my mother not to serve him liver ever.
He had seen them in the raw—
dislocated, discolored, cancerous and cracked—
would never again view them in any other light.

168

Decades later, my mother still
　relished telling this vignette
　　every time she ate her liver
　　　savoring every morsel
　　　　long after he left her
　　　　　and four little girls
　　　　　　just as suddenly as
　　　　　　　he stopped loving her liver.

Sylvia Ramos Cruz

E-pistle

From: Esse@Perplexed.me
To: Emme@Paradox.you

Emme,
Wow! I don't know what to say. Your words leave me speechless.
I've never met you face to face but worked with you once you said
you worked with Elle, someone else whom I have never met
but connected with online as a fellow activist for women's rights.
We helped polish your speech for Women's Equality Day
putting aside other demands on our attention.

Perhaps we were tardy in our response to your final draft but
that doesn't warrant your subsequent e-mail in which you say
women like to lose and fail, refuse to act to guarantee their rights,
waste time with pontificating pretense, are backstabbing,
narcissistic,
petty and jealous, have never helped you, and are most
responsible for the absence of any gender equality in the US.

It's hard to know what caused that barrage to flow from your
keyboard
turn you from comrade-in-arms to puzzling paradox. True,
neither Elle
nor I are paragons of feminist virtue, but neither are we women
not to be trusted, wasting our time in the pursuit of other's
misery, loving
our place as second class citizens, or even lacking a tender heart.
I really don't know what to make of it. It's unsettling!

On second thought, it is unsettling to make connections in the
ether,
form tight bonds with humans we may never look in the eye,
work earnestly on a common cause with strangers,
even lay our aspirations at their virtual feet. Yet,
in this enormous chamber called Universe,

I shout out many times daily, hold my breath as my sound
becomes immersed in the cacophony of billions,
wait to hear it returned transformed and transforming.

Which is why I won't send this e-mail.
Your voice, materializing from the void,
left me speechless.

Yours in sisterhood,
Esse

Sylvia Ramos Cruz

Sisepuede

Si se puede - Yes, it is possible.

Little clay horse
you bring to mind my sister, Esther
digging out of a lifetime
of big and small miseries

Miserias that blow after blow
drove her adolescent dreams
into the ground until they, too,
turned on her asking,
"What right had you to give us life
when there was nothing to nourish us?"

The loss of her *sueños* hurts more
than beatings and beratings.
She knows them both; knows
how they feel on her head, breast, heart;
how they leave raw, red gashes that run deep silent
like polluted streams bleeding into her memories.

Little clay pony
you remind me of the Zuni fetish
I bought Esther on the Turquoise Trail—
a midnight magic horse
imbued with strength enough for two.

She named it *Sisepuede*
said it reminded her of a tiny Somali
girl in her fifth grade class who
when faced with a new task recited
a phrase to herself over and over
in a language so foreign
its intonation seemed incantation.

When Esther asked, "What does she say?"
the girl's older brother said in careful English
"My sister says, I can do this".

172

Margaret Randall

I Do Not Bow My Head

I do not bow my head. Maybe years ago
but these days
when someone commands
let us bow our heads or *observe a moment of silence*
and all chins drop and eyes lower,
I hold mine high,
unwilling to honor the fictitious power.

Celebrate, yes. Submit, no.
Sometimes I close my eyes,
no gesture of reverence but journey
inward to my core.
I do not deny
the deep place others hold in me
or refuse tribute to children or mentors,
those connections that have made me strong.

I do not deny my smallness either
or pretend I am anything
more than one aging woman
born almost eight decades ago
straddling centuries and questions.
Slowly, over that minute or two,
I straighten my shoulders,
refuse to bend my knees
in humbled posture.

Instead, I lift my chin, stand tall,
sure there is nothing and no one
up there, out there, anywhere
but here
in this fierce energy

Margaret Randall

La Llorona

It should come as no surprise.
I found her
by the banks of the San Antonio.
I know, you'd think she'd choose
the Rio Grande or Colorado
for her nightly walks:
rivers of strength and purpose,
dividing nations or raging
through the greatest canyon of them all.
But I knew
she preferred more intimate beauty.
I'd done my homework.

I almost didn't hear her whispered wail
between the moan of freight trains
charging night
in that south Texas city.
I thought I discerned a minor key,
high harmony in late September
and followed the sound
notebook in hand,
sharpened pencil ready.

Around the bend she sat alone,
magnificent profile
hidden beneath her long black veil
I confused at first
with tree shadows in quiet air.
Almost midnight,
still high nineties.
Who could sleep?
I thought she might run
but she turned

slowly toward me,
seemed resigned to talk.

Gain her confidence: oral historian's trick
before sympathy heated my blood
and for one brief moment
I felt what she felt
so many centuries before.
Do you mind if I sit, I trembled,
and she gave me to understand
scorn is a lonely companion,
she'd like the company.
Even legends
endure mistaken identity.

Fearful she'd fade in this Texas heat
I opened with the questions
I knew my readers wanted answers to:
Were you poor but beautiful?
Rich but ugly?
Or did you embody some other mix
of class and magnetism?
Did he come from afar
or was he someone
you played with as a child? You know,
before the era's gender roles kept you apart?

And, I took a breath, *let's talk*
about the children
—I know it must still be painful—
but there's no getting around it,
people want to know.
Did you drown them yourself

or was it someone else
pinned the crime on you?
Their father? Some other authority?

I knew I was breaking every journalistic rule
of free-world impartiality,
feeding questions,
imposing twenty-first century assumption
on this seventeenth century woman
who raised one slender hand
and brushed her veil aside.
A full moon infused her copper skin.
Eyes I'd expected puffy and red
pierced mine.

You've got to understand, she began,
her voice the rustle
of a thousand Sandhill Cranes,
we had few choices when I was alive.
It was marriage
or spend the rest of your days
serving father and brothers.
And yes, she leaned forward,
her face almost touching mine,
the rancid stench of wet leaves

penetrating my nostrils
as I steadied notebook,
struggled to breathe,
why keep it a secret after all this time:
my sort of beauty wasn't praised—
large nose and ears,
a few extra pounds,

fuzzy shadow smudging my upper lip,
eyes that saw too much.
I wanted out . . . no, no, erase that:
I had to escape or I'd have gone mad.

I know people say I was mad
but I was a woman with her life
and we didn't live long
back then,
one life I wasn't going to spend
with a man who only came home
tired of his latest fancy
and reeking of pulque,
how I recoiled at the sickening stench.

I loved my two little boys, of course I did,
Benjamín and Ceferino,
yes they had names
and I want you to name them,
all these years and no one's bothered to ask.
I loved my children and
I'll tell you now I tried to save them,
entered the river
though I couldn't swim,
struggled until water and reeds
threatened to pull me under,
watched the current carry their bodies away.

Why not proclaim my innocence?
I didn't expect that from you,
thought you smarter than to ask,
you must know we can talk and talk
and they still believe

only what fits the stories they write
to keep us under control.
Hysteric, they would have cried,
liar or worse.
Stories written long before my time
and I see nothing has changed that much.

Is that enough? She rose
and let the veil fall
across her dissolving face,
started to turn in resignation or disgust.
But maybe it was something in my eyes.
We were two women talking,
unperturbed by the distance
that separates her time from mine,
roles of historian and informant
long forgotten.

She offered one last smile
and I saw a glimmer
of sympathy
as if I was the twisted legend
and she the poet
destined to set the record straight.
Before she disappeared for good
among the oak and fruitless mahogany
she touched my hand.

Maybe in another hundred years, she said,
if our Mother hasn't devoured us all
and spit us back to space by then.

Margaret Randall

Lay Lady Lay*

Lay Lady Lay, or rise and do your job.
I dream a new Lady, six feet tall
plus whatever it takes
for ships to discern her crown and lifted arm
in a harbor determined to welcome all.

She wears a short leather jacket
and 9-inch spike heels,
size-12 in glistening red patent leather,
carefully plucked eyebrows
on a face where pain has morphed to rage.

Instead of a torch she holds a scale:
two balanced trays hanging from chains
swinging in bay breeze,
describing justice.
Their contents emerge from shameful shadow.

One tray holds the barbwire fence that wept
at Matthew Shepherd's last desperate plea
to live. It bleeds
beside Caster Semenya's running shoes,
all those frightened gasps for air.

The other, still swinging higher,
struggles to hold identity's arc,
a family welcome mat,
warm embrace and smiles
that come before it is too late.

Lay Lady lay, why wait any longer
for the world to begin?
Do your 21st century job for those
whose passionate hearts
are unafraid of difference.

---

* Bob Dylan song

Margaret Randall

Without Warning

At the bus stop and out of the corner of my eye
I see myself waiting,
awkward bundle at my feet.
I am wearing the same sky blue fleece
though it hangs looser against my body.
My hair, still long and full and brown,
frames the younger me in her oblivion.

I swerve and almost hit the car to my right,
snap my neck
to get one last glimpse of myself
before people I loved
took what wasn't theirs,
a child stopped calling home,
and temperature threatened my planet.

Without warning I make a U-turn
and slow way down
to observe every detail
of my younger self.
I even consider a shouted question
might bring an answer
against all mathematical odds.

She looks straight at me and smiles.
I smile back
and keep on driving,
hoping to keep
my appointment with myself.

Georgia Santa Maria

Letter From My Great-Grandmothers to the Macho-Boys of Politics

I.

Maggie Mae : 13 children
Frank, Eddie, Sarah, Maggie, Bessie, James, Georgia, Louise,
William, Harry, David, Evelyn, Frances

It wasn't that I meant to kill myself–it's just
that having 13 children is enough.
The baby is only 6 months old,
and I'm 42, and tired.
James is off working,
building railroads around the World.
And, sometimes I think he only comes home
to get me pregnant again.
I won't!
But he won't take "no".
Sure, the older girls help,
but they're busy too.
I want them to go to college.
become teachers, so they won't
end up like me,
depending on men
for what they need.
I want them to have their freedom.
To earn their own money.
To not be burdened, used, and worn-out
with child-bearing before they're 40.
So I stuck that wire up in my womb.
God, it hurt!
I couldn't stop bleeding.
It took me 6 days to die–
I couldn't stop screaming.
My poor kids, who had to hear me.

Their angry father, telling everybody
I died in "childbirth".
What a truthful lie!
Now, I suppose,
my girls will have to raise
their siblings. But, maybe
my screaming will stay in their minds
and they will be teachers,
celibate, and free.

II.
Catherine: 4 children
Marie, Irene, Morris, Jean

I thought I'd die when he was killed.
On Good Friday, like Jesus,
without the promise of return.
He was only 35.
I was 33.
Our youngest child, not yet born
will never know him. The others,
fourteen, six and twelve,
will have some memories.
But, for all that, it's his absence
they will remember most.
Thank God he left me well-fixed.
A brewery to run, and
apartments to rent out.
We'll have enough money.
The children will be educated well
and cared for adequately.
I will not consider, in light of this all,
marrying again, giving up

my independence, and my money.
I won't be like those other women, buried
in men and dozens of children.
My kids are good. Three girls, one boy.
I'll teach them to always have
their own money.
To be strong in the world.
Independent, like me.

III.
Rose Lee: 6 children
Olivia, Frances, Theodore, Edward, Harry, Lawrence

I couldn't ever catch my breath–
literally, and figuratively.
Every time I had a child
another came along, right behind.
Six in twelve years.
My last at twenty nine.
I was married at eighteen.
The only thing to slow it down
was the tuberculosis
that has now killed me.
My youngest child is only three
My oldest is thirteen.
Not yet a woman, but
not enough behind, herself
with all these little siblings.
Little Harry's sick like me
and may not live.
He has TB.
Coughs all night.
The doctor said he got it from me,

was maybe born with it.
Thank God his little brother,
Larry isn't sick. He was born healthy.
But now I'm dead at thirty two.
My children will be raised
by former slaves of the family,
or sent to boarding schools,
But not by me.

IV.
Fannie: 15 children
James (died), George, James, Alexander (died), Alloch, Victor
(died), Emma, Irene, Otis, Harry, Gerald, Ruthie (died), Orilla,
Baby (died), Baby (died)

It's amazing how much love you have,
still, even for the ones who died.
When my first was born dead I thought
maybe God wouldn't let me have more.
But then, they came–another and another
every year or two. I can't remember
a time when I wasn't pregnant
and nursing on sore tits.
Cleaning them up and
dressing them down–
They get away from me now,
with their pinching and fighting.
Like their father,
a meanness of the spirit
a need for drink.
I had no idea what an outlaw he was.
I thought he was romantic.
A girl can be seduced with stories

and handsome looks.
I fancied him dashing.
Now, he dashes me
if I open my mouth to disagree.
Or some days, just because.
I've tried saying "no" to his advances.
To make some time between pregnancies.
But, then he just goes after the maid
and other girls. God knows
how many other siblings
my kids have scattered
across this windy prairie.
He thinks it's funny.
It's been 3 years now,
since my last dead baby–
longer than any time before.
I'm hoping maybe I'm done–no more.
Nine is enough, with six already in the ground.
Though, I cry every day for my poor lost Ruthie
who got diphtheria when she was four.
I remember the spun-gold of her hair,
her smell, the sweetness
of her soul.

Georgia Santa Maria

The Vegan Feminist Dilemma

The contest calls for poetry from a "Vegan Feminist"
       perspective–
The daily non-sequitur selection from the spin-cage of the web,
the planetary revolve of possibilities. Might just as well have been
"Carnivorous Pederasts" or "The Omnivores Of Dominance,"
addressing the eating habits of sexual politics:
What do we eat in bed?
The obvious answer, of course: Each other. Though that,
removed a pace from Global Warming, or PETA,
or Max Factor's testing labs. The ranch-lands of Wyoming:
Can cowboys be feminists? Perhaps, an anthology called
"Feminists on Horseback." You want a banana with that?
Wyoming granted suffrage fifty years ahead of the US Congress,
Utah shortly after that. Neither state known for being Vegan.
Or, these days, feminist. Does meat put hair on your chest?
Do bean-sprouts cause equal pay-checks?
Does celery help girls with their math?
Will there be fewer unwanted pregnancies if we eat more tofu?
Headline: "With The Aid Of Pineapple, The Glass Ceiling Was
       Cracked."
"Executive Credits Brown Rice with Promotion."
Confusing the contents of our stomachs with
the contents of our lives, uteruses, and heads:
Are six-inch spike heels any less vicious made of plastic?
Do men run faster wearing leather loafers?
Does it do a girl advantage to be foot-bound and emaciated?
Gives her a slim chance for fighting back, or climbing upward.
Why are we perpetually faced with idiotic choices, like:
"Should I eat, or just *become* a vegan tart?" and,
"What *am* I made of, but meat?"

Georgia Santa Maria

I Stand Accused of Hating Men...

and laughing.
I've demonstrated
through a lifetime
Loving Them.
Sometimes, to my own detriment.
Three husbands, lots of boyfriends,
three sons, three grandsons, male friends.
It's just that, with all that close proximity,
I feel entitled to some opinions.
If I were a wildlife expert
who'd spent fifty-odd years
living intimately with lions,
would you grant me any less
than a status of "Specialist?"

Georgia Santa Maria

For the Girls Who Think They're Immune

The biology of birthing hasn't changed:
Have a baby, and you're in it, 20 years.
Love a man, and maybe, he'll do the dishes,
but you're paddling upstream against
the current of at least ten thousand years,
(in a world where women, still, are killed
for the absence of a hymen.)
Men can leave, yet, the species still continues—
on your pelvic bones and moral obligations.
Nevertheless, he may
wash a load of laundry, at least when it's his.
And provided that you're pleasing to him,
thin and smart enough, willing for kinky sex
when your feet are tired,
and you've dealt with fighting kids.
Oh, yeah! You newer generation girls have got it made,
mostly.
And, now for that "glass-ceiling"
son-of-a-bitch.

Georgia Santa Maria

Reasons this Poem is Late

My house burned down.
I couldn't find a pen.
I couldn't find any paper.
My computer got wet from the firemen.
I went to Berlin with my best friend.
My camera survived, so I took photographs.
My husband is a pain in the ass.
He can hardly breathe,
so he needs
all the available oxygen in my world.
My life is taking care of him
and the house,
and the dogs,
and our stuff,
and the money,
and the emotional well being of
fill in the blank with your name.

Elaine Schwartz

Ars Poetica: the writing group

women writers are wonderful
they fill the teapot
turn the spigot off
keep the water boiling

a warm room
a mindful teacher
a cup of soothing hot tea
a safe harbor for the muse

Elaine Schwartz

Leaving for university

There she stands
faded floral apron neatly tied
paring knife in her right hand
a yellow onion held firmly in the left
she peels it with great precision
    golden skin falling to the kitchen counter
    followed by layers of translucent flesh

    Onion crescents slipping from her fingers
    she mutters, *onion tears*
    turns her back to me

    Later, driving north on the old coast road,
    I remember the onion
    her hand grasping the slippery core
    not letting go

Elaine Schwartz

Gaza

What is so compelling as the eyes of a child?
Crossing the green line of innocence, the eyes of a child

Cluster bombs scatter willfully across the schoolyard
Bring a deadly game of hopscotch to the eyes of a child

Grains of white desert sand sift through broken fingers
Measure time until bullets silence the whys of a child

Ancient tongues proclaim the death knell of olive trees
Pomegranates bleed through the milky sighs of a child

The village tailor sews bones together again and again
Baskets of figs bring moon-silver delight to the eyes of a child

The pregnant white mare canters across the village square
Her steaming nostrils caress the wind-tossed sighs of a child

Hold tight the ancient house key, the well worn walking stick
Leather sandals stir the dust but cannot mute the cries of a child

The crescent moon sheds silent grace upon the village ruins
And you, Esther, are lost in the questioning eyes of a child

Elaine Schwartz

Letter to my sister on the southern shore

Do you remember?
Two young sisters snuggling in the valley
of a sway back mattress.
Soft brown lashes grazing your cheeks.
My child's voice guiding you to dreamland.

> *Hey diddle diddle*
> *The cat and the fiddle*
> *The cow jumped over moon,*
> *the moon, the moon . . .*

Tonight, beneath the full moon,
the bay is a blanket of silver,
the only one we now share.
I on the northern shore,
you on the southern,
grandchildren at our knees,
nursery rhymes on our tongues.
Between us, only silence.

Elaine Schwartz

Dear Mother,

Is that you standing in the doorway of the summer cottage,
wrapped in a beach towel, white gardenia pinned to your
flowing black hair? Your dark eyes glow beyond the faded
photo as you glance into the distance and smile.
Oh, Mother, such a smile, the likes of which I've never
seen on your face.
I wish I had known you then.

Jasmine Sena y Cuffee

Wife of God

Imagine a long
white tied
tunic birdcage dress

it hangs
in the lobby of heaven
remembers
woman's flesh
and touch of man

weaved with rope,
yarn,
and canvas strips

it's the anatomy
of a dress
tornado of fabric
tamed
by a wind tunnel
weaver's hands meant
to clothe the sun

it's an Empress's
gown
to greet the dawn

cocoon ribcage
of thrown
away things
she wears driftwood
and seaweed
broken
branch

birch blooming
insides and splintered bone.

We keep ourselves caged
in trappings we can't
wiggle out from
let our dress define us
cause it says something
when we
stand in it
like this

We hold ourselves
straight
and steady one foot
in front
of the next

shimmy and sashay
show off our curves
in the light
perk up
the breasts
blush
the cleavage

We create like this
and dance like this
slender and smooth
bare-legged
and hold chaste
for those
that deserve it

193

keep our power
in pouches
tucked under the rib cage
and prove Goddess like this

Decide to use our strength
when we are ready
when we have to
when we have prepared well

We fight
to be seen and heard
dangle
from projected images
and redefine
ourselves through objects
but there are those
who quiver
when we say
we bring forth
life.
A light
blinding to those who stare
too long and don't
revere its knowing

I choose
to bind myself
and unbind myself
at the whims
of my heart strings
call me Sophia

Solomon's attempt to
resurrect
the temple was only a feat
of my closet

something to wear
and worship my body.

I chose you to become god

wrapped you in my knowledge
and told you
listen I will teach you
eat from me,
drink from me, envy my lines
perfect

I will hold reserve you
let you stare at my brilliance
and tether me
here for remembering

in turn,
you will reveal
everything
strip naked
before me and sing
I herald souls from the earth
to the divine

call me Destroyer
call me Baphomet
I wear this white dress for you.

Marilyn Stablein

Bosque Sand Sculpture

Gather wood of juniper
for the torso, river-washed
twine binds cotton wood
spine. Atop river clay mask

salt cedar sprig headdress
rustles, hums desert breeze.
Obsidian arrowhead eyes
reflect cumulus sky ciphers.

Found broken wood ruler
for good measure. Rusty cans
to string into arms and legs;
road runner feather fingers jut

from swallow's nest palms.
Pictograms indent wet sand.
Songline hymns of the ancients
course through our grateful bones.

Marilyn Stablein

Desert Amulet

Peel bark of mulberry,
soak till the fibers split.
Pound to a pulp with river stone,
siphon water through porous mesh.
Dry the pulp to form sheets.

For ink grind dried petals
of purple iris or peeled walnut
husks. Add water, ferment
in the sun until pigment runs thick.
Carve a quill pen from pheasant
feather gathered in the bosque.

In winter when the sun rides low
write the praises you silently sing
when the moon fills. Stitch what
you gathered, molded and saved as
the poem's offering. Lay humble
amulet in the *nicho* of abundance.

Marilyn Stablein

Harvest Seed Ritual

Weave a pouch from dried palm
fibers. Fill with seeds gathered
each fall: squash, melon, chili,
white and blue corn, tomato, pinto,
foods of spirit and sustenance.

Keep seed pouch in a high, dry place.
Plant each spring in arable moistened soil
after the late frosts retreat. Pray for rain,
replenish the land. Harvest and feast
then gather seeds to store in a safe place.

Every year repeat the ritual. Store
the bounty to sustain seasons
of famine and neglect. Share with
neighbors and enemies, both.
Pray, eat for a hundred seasons.

Cynthia West

Shame

Raped, my body disappeared, hidden
even from my dreams. With my blossom broken,
how could I reach my root? Tears
from my ruined rose flowed down my legs.

Hidden even from my dreams, folded away,
blood guilt cried what my mind could not accept.
Tears from my ruined nest ran down my legs.
Alone at home, fear blocked any easing of

the loss my mind could not accept.
There was nothing I could eat with my mouth
closed by shame. Alone, I stayed home refusing
to look up. In the night inside my womb,

I drew wet wings, a hungry beak. Who could
want me with my flower sealed by wounds?
Yet the cave of my retreat demanded
I crawl out, be indecently exposed.

The darkness of my womb is all I've saved,
with my blossom broken, I can't make any fruit.
When I was raped my body disappeared.
Yet I must crawl out, be indecently exposed.

Cynthia West

Our Drums

For we are the women
we are the daughters
we are the mothers
we are the grandmothers.

For we sing with our waters
sing life into flower
call the roots to drink
cause the berries to ripen.

For our waters are light
for our branches are greening
on their journey
toward fruit.

For we are the prayers
for we are the ancestors
for we are those yet to come
for we are the moon.

For we sing with our waters
for we are the sun
for we give thanks with our tears
for we give thanks with our corn.

For we give thanks
with our drums
for we have lost much
for we have found much.

For we are the women
we are the healers
we are the artists
we are the colors of life.

Cynthia West

To My Children

The same one as always, I sit,
  aged now under the grape vines,
  but no older than before.
My boughs have stretched
  as wide as my roots have drunk.
  Watering with the hose, feeding
  your dry places, there was no counting
  the leaves your small hands tossed to the sun.

Motherless, I became a parent
  by eating what I found in the desert,
  the wide open sky, scant drops of rain,
  any bitter herb.
In my caring there were no nights,
  no days, just the hummingbird
  caught in bare hands and miles
  of moon-lit sage.

With no door and no concern,
  I held your bodies when it snowed,
  soothed your sorrows with drums
  and songs. It seemed there was never
  enough food, yet we laughed
  as we cried. What I didn't know how to give
  didn't bother you, young candles
  too bright to care.
Today, I see myself standing in you,
  broken and whole, at once.

Cynthia West

To My Daughter

I held your small hand,
   read to you,
      turned you step by step   to learn my dance,
         the one I thought best for you.

I lifted your face up,   up, like the rising branches
   until I thought you could swallow the sun
      by yourself. I admired
   the hopes I'd pasted on you,   planning
     for you to complete

my idea of fruit.   Too busy whirling
   to my own music   I didn't notice
     my clouds had failed   to provide
          the sort of rain you could drink.
    Little I guessed your tree
        needed another earth

than mine, another water
   to grow strong   against
      the killing frosts.

Cynthia West

To My Daughter Let Yourself Receive

The countless acts of tenderness
you carelessly dropped
like worn-out clothes
that didn't matter. They are here
to remind you that
you have built a bright-colored house
with windows glancing welcome,
with a smiling door. Alive with flowers,
it waits for you to enter,
to eat the food
you prepared. Forget your worthlessness.
Your giving has formed a haven,
brick by brick. It contains mountains,
rivers and eagles. Find the path
you raked staying up soothing the sick.
The faces of your love
have prepared a celebration
for your return, so you can receive
the halls you polished,
the warm carpets you wove,
the ripened grapes
you planted long ago.

Holly Wilson

Stupid Men

This is what you're missing:
Going down on your woman,
feeling her muff hair
caress your cheeks,
feeling her thighs
squeeze around your face,
feeling her roll and moan
as the tip of your tongue wags
back and forth across her clit,
standing erect in front of you,
making her come
You taste her juices flowing out
readying her even more
to receive you

This is what you're missing:
after enjoying your woman
from the front, back, sideways,
sitting, kneeling, laying down,
you can't hold out anymore
and you positioned yourself
to give her your best penetration
And as all of your manhood
erupts inside of her
your pelvis pushes down on hers
making her erupt, too,
paralyzed for that suspended moment,
clinging as you come together
In a lingering embrace

Yes, that is what you're missing,
you who have convinced them
that it will keep them away

from temptation,
and not disgrace the family honor,
it is a rite of passage
a woman must go through –
your mothers and aunts
had the same thing done
when they were your age,
your husband will be much happier
to see it more "tidy" down there

Ten-year-old girl
dress pulled up around her face,
underwear pulled off,
legs spread apart,
screaming, struggling
begging for you not to do it

Her blood curdling cries
muffled by the women holding her down,
as the piece of broken glass, razor blade
slices off
her human dignity
as you rape her
with your self-righteousness

You who give this small piece of flesh
so much power
that you think it
better to remove
the source of your discontentment
than to take a chance
that your woman would
spread her legs willingly

and gladly give it to you,
and that you could feel great joy
in taking it from her

Yes, that is what you're missing,
it is you who have chosen
to make yourself impotent
of ever truly being able
to please your woman
or feel this holy union with her –

Stupid men!

Tanaya Winder

I am not murdered. I am not missing.
A Lament for Loretta and the Disappeared

for the murdered and missing Indigenous women in the world

When searching for the missing remember 4 things:
Never lose faith. For in it lies our hope like a seed ready to sprout change.

824.
There are now more than 824 missing and murdered aboriginal girls and women in Canada
There are more girls and women missing in other countries too.
Our sisters are missing.
824 spirits we can hear longing to come home.

Every Valentine's Day, indigenous women, their families and their allies rally across the country to remember those girls and women whose cases have gone unsolved and in many cases uninvestigated.

Loretta was 26 years old and many of the other girls and women I don't know....their names or how old they are.

Do we see their faces plastered on posters with the word
MISSING
Yes, we are *missing* you all. We are *missing* our sisters. We miss you. Come home.

Somewhere a mother and father are missing their daughter. Brothers and sisters miss their sister. Nephews and nieces miss auntie. Someone is missing his or her mom.
Someone is missing.

I am not murdered. I am not missing

And so I will speak even to those who won't listen.
I will speak because
I am not murdered. I am not missing
I am one part of a thread of voices
Of bodies or women standing up to speak for those who are
murdered
Those who are missing
Those whose families are missing them
We are here to support our stolen sisters
Young native girls and aboriginal women

Aboriginal Canadian women are 5 times more likely to be
violently attacked than non-aboriginal women

It ends here.

Our children shouldn't grow up having to fear being murdered
or kidnapped
They shouldn't be born into risk, afraid to walk down the street.
So this isn't just a call to action but a demand to end the violence.
A calling to only treat our women with love and respect.

They may have taken their bodies but we shall remember and
speak their names

Where are our sisters? Where are our sisters?
We are our sisters. Remember. Bring them home.
We won't forget and we won't stop speaking.
Bring them home.

When searching for the missing remember 1 thing:

It ends here.

photo from along old Route 66 by Karen Koshgarian

Kenneth P. Gurney

Homecoming

The kids ride their bicycles up and down the street.
Their faces twist from angelic to demonic
as they alternate laughing and screaming.
They chase the roaming dog that barks and barks
until the pooch locates relief on my porch
where I sit on the glider.

In the background a siren wails its emergency
and a dropped ice cream cone melts
and runs toward the sewer grating
where a crumpled twenty-four ounce soda cup
daggers the iron ribs.

A soldier recently returned from Afghanistan
sits on the curb in front of my house.
He places his hands over his ears
and counts out loud: he is up to seventy-two.
His face displays three days beard growth.
He is fully aware of every sound in the neighborhood,
even the gentle wing-flaps of the butterflies.
Sometimes he stands and salutes the invisible.
Sometimes he ducks in-coming mortar rounds.

The kids ignore him.

Earlier in the day, I walked the old Glorieta battlefield*
where the sun struck me like a heavy-weight's punches
and the dusty wind sandpapered my skin.
I felt something else there:
the jerking shadows and haunting echo
of the Fourth Texas Mounted Rifles' advance
toward Pigeon's Ranch
and the flutter of their banners in the wind.

The soldier turns away from the bicycling kids in the street

and walks up to my porch steps.
"Is that your dog?" he says pointing.
"I've seen that dog's face somewhere before.
Come here boy!" But the dog runs away.

---

*The Battle of Glorieta Pass, New Mexico Territory, took place from March 26-28, 1862, and was the decisive battle of the Civil War in New Mexico, as the invading Confederate forces were defeated by Union forces and prevented from going further west.

León Felipe

1939*

Oh this pain,
this pain of having no more tears;
this pain
of not having enough weeping
to water the dust.
Oh, this weeping for Spain,
that now is nothing more than furrow and drought...
Grimace,
austere grief of the land,
under a rainless sky,
crankshaft hiccup
over an empty pit,
mechanism, without tears!
Oh this Spanish grimace,
this dramatic and grotesque grin!

Weeping dry dust
and for the dust...
for the dust of all the things ended in Spain
for the dust of all the dead
and all the ruins of Spain...
for all the dust of a
people now lost in History forever!

Dry weeping of dust
and for the dust. For the dust
of a house without walls,
a tribe without blood,
eye-sockets without tears,
furrows without water...
Dry dusty weeping
for the dust that doesn't join together any more,
neither for the construction of an adobe
nor to raise hope.

Oh! Yellow cursed dust
that brought us rancor and pride
of centuries
and centuries
and centuries...
Because this dust is not from today,
nor from somewhere else:
we are all desert and African

Sandy un-irrigated land,
flesh crushed without tears,
rebellious dust of rancorous rocks
and enemy lavas,
yellow and sterile atoms
of barrenness,
vengeful angles,
sandlot of envy...
Wait there dry and forgotten
until the sea overflows.

---

*The title-date "1939" refers to the end of the Spanish Civil War (1936-39) and the year Fascist General Francisco Franco triumphed over the elected government of the Second Republic, with the help of Hitler and Mussolini, killing close to a million people in the process. León Felipe (1884-1968) left Spain in 1938, shortly before the collapse of the Republic and went into exile in Mexico. He had fought in the Republican Army and was a well known leftist poet. This poem shows his pessimism and sadness at the defeat and is taken from J.M. Castellet's anthology *Un Cuarto de Siglo de Poesia Española* (Barcelona, Seix Barral, 1966, pp. 117-118). Translation by GLB.

Donald Levering

Notes from the Button Accordion

The problem is too many hands.

Nina presses the chipped buttons,
her kids dancing for tips
from the idlers in the line
that weaves around the block
of shuttered storefronts.

Strained faces give way to relief.
A few dig into pockets.
Nickels and pennies chink
in Nina's busker can.

Hands knocking on doors.
Hands folded in prayer.
Smoking hands.

No matter how sweat-stained or tattered,
each man in line is wearing a hat–
bowler, fedora, pork pie, or mickey's cap.
It is, to be sure, 1931.

This time through the song and dance
Nina's kids have holey shoes.
This ditty's for the soup kitchen queue.

Nina squeezes the refrain
and her children shuffle and kick.
A drunk joins them clumsily
and people hoot.
A cop on his beat calls the kids *monkeys*.

◎   ◎   ◎

The problem is not enough jobs.

Guthrie crooned about the families
on relief. Mother counted *food stamps.*
Dad growled *handouts.*
Talk show demagogues repeat
Cadillac driving welfare queens.

How many queens playing polkas
on chipped accordions?
How many foregone hopes
hopping freight trains?

Hands picking apples.
Hands clipping hedges.
Hands scrubbing floors.
Hands changing diapers.

◎   ◎   ◎

The problem, we're told on TV,
is bad genes. Poor esteem.
Unlucky rolls of the dice.
The issue is missed opportunity.
Credit risk. Miserly tips. Hard knocks.

This time through the crash,
financiers jump
with golden parachutes.
This time bankers claiming bonuses.
How much friction
does it take to make a blister?
How many turns of the same screw
to make a factory shift?

This time in the queue to the benefits office
we pass the mural on the pawn shop wall

where Our Lady of the Missing Paycheck
extends her palms for alms.

Instead of Nina's grandchild
here to play a squeezebox tune,
a passing clunker strafes booming bass.
It is, after all, Twenty-Fourteen.

When we edge to the front of the line,
the caseworker calls it *temporary*.

The problem is toxic bonds.
Leveraged debt. Homes foreclosed.
The problem is record profits.

Callused hands of the gardener.
Chapped nanny hands.
Hands that smell of vinegar.
Hammer-bruised fingers.

Donald Levering

To My Son, Grown Older in the Woods

All night you couldn't sleep for the elk
gnawing on the aspens' bark outside your tent.
At dawn you rose to find your car
with two flat tires riven with roofing tacks.

You hiked hot miles to the last house
you'd driven past.
                    Trees inside the fence
were hung with signs warning away
Niggers, Jews, and *Gov't Agents.*

Closer to the house were strung mutilated effigies
of sombreroed Mexicans, robed Arabs
with forehead targets, Hillary Clinton
with gouged-out breasts.
                         Charged by three dogs
you kept at bay with a stick, you backed away.
By luck their master wasn't home.

Back on the road you discovered
          he'd painstakingly set up
          hundreds of roofing tacks.
The woods warped in the heat.

Against utter evil what can I tell
you, what fatherly wisdom?

Remember reading *Baba Yaga,*
          whose forest house stood on chicken feet,
          with travelers' skulls on fenceposts?
          She forced captive children to scrub floors
          under threat of being eaten alive.

I hope you always will dwell
with the rest of the story,

how the boy's kindness to animals and trees
was rewarded in his escape;
how two Spanish-speaking men
gave you a lift and drove hours out of their way
to get your tires fixed
and your faith restored.

Saeb:
Three Hundred Thousand Persian Couplets/ Ghazals*

Quite a few years ago, I happened upon Coleman Barks' presentation of the poetry of Rumi (Jalal al-Din Rumi, died 1273), first in some of his books of Rumi's poetry rendered into English (e.g. *The Essential Rumi*), then later I saw him with a coterie of musicians on PBS giving a Rumi reading with musical back-up. He's good! Later, I was animated to see the touring Mevlevi Order of Sufi Dervishes dancing/whirling to the poetry of Rumi at UCLA. Barks doesn't know Persian or Farsi but counts on his Sufi teacher and the translations of others (plus his ability as a poet) to give meaning to Rumi's work. For 30 years Barks taught in the English Department at the University of Georgia. Poet Robert Bly and Sudanese musician Hamza al-Din have both collaborated with Barks. Rumi, who is claimed by both Iran and Afghanistan, has probably become the most well known Middle Eastern poet in the U.S. since Lebanese poet Khalil Gibran (1883-1931), or maybe Palestinian poet Mahmoud Darwish (1941-2008). But if any American can think of a Middle Eastern poet today, it would probably be Rumi. However, there were other Persian poets of note in earlier centuries, and, although Saeb (or Saib, 1601-77) lived much later than Rumi, he was as well known in his own time as the great Sufi poet. (Saeb himself was Shi'a). Another versifier whom many may know is Persian poet Hafiz (Shams ud-Din Mohammed Hafiz, 1320-1389) through a book of translations by Daniel Ladinsky (*The Gift: Poems by Hafiz, the Great Sufi Master*). Saeb is apparently in the qualitative category of Hafiz and Rumi, though from a later period.

While reading the poetry of the great Spanish poet Federico Garcia Lorca (1898-1936) many years ago, I came across some of his poems that were labeled as poems from a tradition I was unfamiliar with: the ghazal (*gacela* in Spanish) and the casida (*casida* in Spanish). I read up on these forms and their contexts and later also found examples of the adapted forms in the work of the major

Argentine poet Leopoldo Lugones (1874-1938). So these forms have moved from Persian and Arabic poetry to western poetry, at least to some extent, and the ghazal is still written today by American and other western poets. As far as Persian is concerned, "It took 2-3 centuries for Persian, an Indo-Aryan language . . . . to assimilate those semitic elements of Arabic origin which enriched its vocabulary and modified its rhetoric." (See Alex Preminger's *Princeton Encyclopedia of Poetry & Poetics*, 1972 edition, p. 609). All Persian poetic meters come from Arabic prosody (except one) and are quantitative. The ghazal, which dates to the 8th Century, varies in length from 5 to 12 couplets, all with the same rhyme. It was German Romantic poets, such as Goethe and Friedrich Schlegel, who introduced the form into western literatures. What the Persians did to the ghazal was to perfect the rhyming couplet and then to use it in long, extensive poetic compositions. An example would be the epic of Persia's first great poet Firdausi (died 1020), whose immense work *Shahnama*, formed of 60,000 rhyming couplets, presented the history of Persia's ancient kings.

Saeb's full name is Mirza Mohammed Ali Saeb Tabrizi, and he was from an Azeri merchant family in Tabriz which later moved to Isfahan. He became not only a master of the ghazal and wrote an estimated 300,000 of them, but also wrote an epic poem titled *The Campaign Against Kandahar*. Often the ghazal form reminds me of the famous Persian "miniatures" in art, which focus on specific scenes like the ghazal, also a sort of miniature. Saeb traveled to Afghanistan, Kashmir and India, where he met the Moghul Emperor Shah Jahan (who built the Taj Mahal).   –GLB

---

*"The ghazal is composed of a minimum of five couplets and typically no more than fifteen-that are structurally, thematically, and emotionally autonomous. Each line of the poem must be of the same length, though meter is not imposed in English. The first couplet introduces a scheme....subsequent couplets pick up the same scheme...the final couplet usually includes the poet's signature, referring to the author in the first or third person....frequently including the poet's own name.." – Definition from the American Academy of Poets online.

The Garden of Amazement:
Saeb and The Ghazal

by Robin MacGowan

Saeb (1590-1676) was the outstanding Islamic poet of his lifetime, celebrated for his jewel-like couplets and a highly innovative "Indian" style that brought an inspiring sparkle and complexity to Persian poetry. But posterity has not treated well a poet whose 7,000 ghazals* far outnumber any other Persian poet. Saeb's long-lived productivity, and the convoluted intricacies of his two-line distichs, have combined to deny a poet–at his best as great as Hafez–the worldwide readership he would seem to deserve.

"It surprises me," Saeb observes, "how scattered remarks, once placed in a book, attain coherence." But aphoristic chaos doesn't automatically become memorable, let alone aesthetically satisfying. An editorial eye has to organize and place the gem-like scatterings.

In partnership with Reza Saberi, I have devised an editorial process to introduce Saeb's poetry to western readers. I have chosen several hundred distichs from Saberi's bilingual text, *Selected Verses from Saeb Tabrizi*, culled from a two-volume Persian edition containing 3,168 ghazals. In adapting Saberi's translations, I have aimed to present a work that makes sense, not as Sufi wisdom, but as poetry. Not an easy task; language that seems clear enough to a metaphysician can require much decoding before the poetic jewels come across in something like their presumed sparkle. The formal means required to turn aphoristic material into verse inevitably distort. This is, therefore, not a translation in the usual sense, but something more like a collage. I have adapted two-line "gems" from Saberi and recombined them by imagistic subject, i.e. the Pearl, the Rose and its entourage of Dewdrop and Nightingales, Wine, Nights and Taverns, the Caged Court-Bird, the questing Road, the apocalyptic Flood. The resulting collage conveys the contours of Saeb's poetic world: the creative pulses propelling it and that rather more hidden subject that emerges from his writing, a richly lived life.

220

Applied to modern poetry's concept of "an organic whole" so rigorously composed that the smallest shift of punctuation can dismantle a poem's intricate balance, such lobotomy would be unthinkable. By what right am I depriving Saeb's reader of the subtle connections and power that accrue, couplet by added couplet, in a rhyme-turned ghazal?

But an organicity that a Western reader takes for granted may not hold in the same measure to work from another time and culture. Western poems proceed by developing consistent multi-leveled arguments line by line. They build towards something: the resolution of a last line, the clarification of a final title. Classic Persian poems, typically untitled, feature a more meditative circling, couplet upon closed couplet, with little more than a rhymed repetition to keep the perimeter from wobbling out of control. Form is more flexible, and far more repetitious than its Western counterpart. Ghazals are written to be sung, or if not sung read aloud, and performers may draw a single syllable out to stunning length, conveying infinite feeling in a hall of mirrors.

Instead of exploring an image, a list, a metaphorical sequence as a Western poet might, Saeb proceeds by a more meditative unburdening. A couplet is finished and cast away, and another is picked up to undergo the same treatment. In the same way the ghazal moves from its charged starting point (the same rhyme word ending the first two lines) toward the dismissive self-reference of the concluding couplet; a kind of theme-and-variations poetry emphasizing the virtues of cleverness, wit, and exuberant play. Direction, such as it is, is hidden. Face to face with poetic mystery–the Unknown Beloved, God himself, if you like–he prefers hermetic discretion. Secrets , like women, are best kept veiled: "Beauty/ strip her as we must/ stays concealed."

These restrictions hold equally well for the pearl-like form of a Persian *bayt* or couplet. In classical poetry the verse unit comprises two hemistichs, each called a *meara*. Unlike the end-stopped Western couplet, which can be broken or enjambed in the interest of a greater whole, the *bayt* commands an inviolable unity all its own:

The couplet that, striking the ear,
fails to enrapture,
    may be less than mature.

Rapture comes, in other words, complete in itself.
Saeb sees himself as a miniaturist, a jeweler fashioning the
pearls of a necklace:

In my book no word stands
unexamined. Their pearls come
            well-
            pierced
            from
            their
            oyster.

These pearl couplets were arranged to be strung, one more
amazing, hopefully, than the last, in the 7-15 (or more) strand that
is a ghazal. But nothing kept them from assuming an excerpted
life of their own, each wobble of a phrase brought out in a song,
or anthologized in one or another *Garden of Amazement*. Whatever
they may have lost in being wrenched out of a less-than-precise
context, they gained in another, equipped for recitation. Bayts
were addressed to a reader-listener's memory. Persians to this day,
from all walks of life, pride themselves on the number of such cou-
plets they can summon at will. Each is his own treasure chest.

Saeb's revolutionary impact on Indo-Persian poetry and such
world-class poets as Bidel and Mirza Ghalib comes from the high-
ly embellished baroque syntax he imparts to this basic two-line
unit. Often, a chain unwinds from within a negative assertion:

Silence does not veil
            a secret's truth. Musk,
    borne from a far room,
                    makes its
                    effects
                    felt.

222

Or, elsewhere in the same ghazal:

Were my feet less entangled
in their bodily mesh
would they find under their soles
sky's red carpet

In Saeb's metaphysical style, the demurral of "were" and "less" create a withheld space within which the second half of the couplet can ascend, from the terrestrial "feet" to the spiritual stratosphere of "sky's red carpet." "Carpet," however, returns the mystical insight to the very feet from whence it began; in a mere two lines, what a trip! In other distichs the heights gained by such syntactical license make room for a Pierrot-like display, a man wonderfully teary, and ever so vulnerable.

The couplet form here is a binary one: it begins with a pithy assertion, "Silence does not veil a secret's truth." Then, seizing on the buried metaphor in the erotic, forbidden aspect of "veil," there follows an almost Schubertian modulation, "Musk, borne from a far room, makes its effects felt." We are not permitted to glimpse the Beauty in her out-of-bounds room. But we certainly feel her erotic impact. To capture such ricocheting reverberations, I have resorted to a stepped line, often fragmented for rhythmic effect. Because Saeb is an intensely spatial poet, as concerned as any contemporary with issues of freedom and flight, the steps into broken vertical space give his condensed articulations the poetic wings it needs.

Two court poets of the previous generation, Fayzi and Urfi, pioneered the "Indian" style Saeb inherited. Their achievement lay in the different ways they played with "metaphors that had become stock poetic devices . . . to take advantage of the metaphors themselves."* Saeb in turn took this several steps further, elevating the metaphors to a point where they became personae for the poet himself, the moth around the candle, the dewdrop and nightingale forever circling about their Rose. Where before the poet stood removed from the figures he evoked, with Saeb, images and poet stand on the same human plane. A couplet becomes a dance of exchanges, between equals. Nor, from a jeweler's perspective, can anything be too small: "Awareness, in a drop of water / discerns the ocean."

As these stock figures reappear in ever more astonishing contexts, they take on a metaphysical complexity. To show the range this takes, I've given a few of them their own ghazal-like stage. The approach resembles one pioneered by the phenomenological critics of the Geneva school: Georges Poulet, Gaston Bachelard, and Jean-Pierre Richard. Like them, I remove the context in which they occur in order to reveal the faceted structure giving life to a great writer's world. I've further shaped it so the reader encounters that invisible thing in Persian poetry, an authentic life, "spent on the line."

The range Saeb invokes is a considerable one, from the pre-natal recollections of "Ocean Days," to the young cleric remembered in his "celibate dungeon," to the elderly man actually welcoming the "roaring waters" of his long-sought final ocean. Along the way we meet in several guises the lover, the wine-bibber, the encaged courtier and bureaucrat, the solitary writer, the restless poet constantly on the move, a man of many different aspects. But they all add up to an unusually long-lived poet who created for himself an inherently interesting life.

* * *

Mirza Mohammad Ali Saeb was born in Tabriz, the capital of Turkish-speaking Azerbaijan province in northwest Iran, the son of a local merchant. In 1603, when Saeb was thirteen or fourteen years old, the family was one of a thousand Azerbaijani families of merchants and craftsmen drafted by Shah Abbas to help in the building of the new Safavid capital in Isfahan.

It is hard to know how to interpret Saeb's ironic self-portraiture, but in "Poisonous Remorse" a picture emerges of a child more than a bit hyper, intensely curious, very much a night owl, and inclined to do things his own eccentric way. Religious schooling, the only kind available to an adolescent male in most Persian communities, saw Saeb assuming the role of an ascetic upon graduation and embarking on the hazardous pilgrimage to Mecca. Disillusion soon followed, disgust with clerical venality and hypocrisy. Then came, if we are to believe "Ocean Days," an awakening not unlike Rumi's, as erotic as it was spiritual. Those "thirsty lips" liberating his "fountain" from its ascetic travertine led Saeb to the mystical Sufi branch of Shiite Islam and the life of a wandering dervish. We spot him in Rumi's Anatolia, in the holy city of Najaf, in Baghdad, and then for a time in northeastern Iran. From the holy city of Mashad he travels, by way of Kabul, to India. There follow two lengthy sojourns in Delhi at the court of Shah Jahan, the patron of the Taj Mahal and a beacon for artists from across the Islamic spectrum.

The four to five years spent in India had a liberating effect on Saeb and the ambition of his poetry. The life of a winebibber he enjoyed at court would not have been so available in Isfahan. Taking advantage of a water-blessed climate, the Moghul emperors and their liegemen built gardens intended as meeting places for sexual intrigue and personal display. India brought also into Saeb's poetry a more diverse stock of imagery: partridges, parrots, snakes; perhaps also a more tightly packed, not to say crammed, aesthetic. Inevitably came a spiritual widening to embrace ideas of karma, and of Hindu-like kinship with a vast spectrum of reincarnated life down to moths and ants. In a culture that catered to gurus, Saeb could become another enlightened mentor, offering advice to one or another befuddled adherent traipsing behind him on the mystical path.

In his poems Saeb doesn't make clear what occasioned his two departures from Shah Jahan's court. Judging from the remarks in "Silent Lips," it is conceivable that a less-than-politic tongue might have made his leaving expedient. He lived, though, in a time of ever-increased political instability, both in Moghul India and Safavid Iran. Having seen the handwriting on Jahan's wall, Saeb may have seen a benefit in returning to Isfahan to become the second Shah Abbas's "king of poets."

Despite all the uncertainty that surrounds his life and and work, Saeb is not, like Hafez, a poet of teasing opacities. Instead he brings into Persian poetry a highly personal "I," using direct self-reference in a way that feels almost Western. Identity is always something very slippery for poets to project and readers to infer; hence in so many the recourse to a mask behind which they feel less naked, less vulnerable. Nor is Saeb immune to offering "pseudo-theosophical" advice that may grate on the modern ear as condescending.

In a world where to say what you thought–about virtually anything–was nothing short of suicidal, Saeb clearly needed his personae, the pearls, nightingales, caged birds, dewdrops even, which he inhabits with such soulful brio. But, side by side with the stock figures, lies a far from conventional self-invention. Saeb relishes recounting the considerable work of personal reconstruction he has undergone, with all its sleights, comeuppances and pratfalls. His gnomic opinions, in other words, are a foil for the display of comic versatility, of how to be poetically outrageous and somehow or other get away with it. Moreover, the bar he raises and insists on jumping over–in a mere two lines!–is one perfectly adapted to the bundle of contradictions he displays. On the one side of the self-portrait we see the outgoing, restless, portly, wine-swilling *bon vivant* and ladies' man, a creature clearly on the side of life. On the other, lurks a more reclusive Pierrot-like Sufi mystic, plaintively insisting that the only life worth cultivating is a tear-drenched inner one.

It's a difficult, not to say impossible, combination to reconcile, but in couplet after couplet, with an admirable straight face that's what we see Saeb attempting. To be able to link, in a two-line miniature form, a sensibility of truly baroque grandeur–even the sky is a quixotic adversary–with a self-referential wit, marks a verve genuinely original. I have collaged these *Scattered Gems* as a showcase for poetry of a highly eccentric comic brilliance.

---

* Marshall G.S. Hodgson, *The Venture of Islam*, v. III, p. 80.

Sky's Red Carpet

754-1, 2, 3, 8
> The concept light-spirited words embody
>> mounts though the sky.
>>> Their eagle soars
>>>> on pinions of carefully
>>>>> culled metaphor.

> No concept can encompass Love's
>> magnitude: the cosmos,
>>> a partridge
>>>> in its raptor's talons.

> Silence doesn't veil
>> a secret's truth. Musk,
>>> borne from a far room
>>>> makes its effects felt.

> Were my feet less entangled
>> in their bodily shroud
>>> would they find under their soles
>>>> sky's red carpet?

The Garden Of Amazement

644-5

> Once I've scrubbed my inner mirror of rust
>> will each orchard leaf reflect
>>> the green of a sweet
>>>> singing lorikeet?

383-8

> Backed, like a mirror, against bedazzlement's wall:
>> the entire rose-garden,
>>> petals and thorns,
>>>> equally astound.

2779-5

Once Enlightenment's garden gate swung open
in every plant I sniff
a whiff of Paradise.

1851-7

If the Unseen's without springs
or gardens, from where, Saeb,
do your kaleidoscopes spring?

Character

667-5

No one looks to improve his character.
We'd all like to improve our looks.

670-9

Comeuppance, survived, recounts well.
In tomorrow's mirror
today's wrinkles look not bad.

403-6, 8

Time and again I've scuttled from prying eyes
yet the streets still teem
with inquisitive police.

I keep going, whatever the guise
even if a handful of straw's
all my fire draws.

2780

Ecstasy's a poultice
for penury's blisters.
But I'd trade both
for a shot of booze.

1796-11

> An orchard branch sags under the weight
>> of its fruit; so does my back
>>> under the shame of its fruitlessness.

1516-3

> My arrow will cleave its bull's eye
>> the day suffering bends my spine
>>> into a bow.

442-8

> When your every mote, Saeb, blew in,
>> borne on contrary gales,
>>> it took the revolving heavens
>>>> more than a day to piece you
>>>>> together.

Breath

9-7

> Strike from the record any hour
>> less than consciously spent.
>>> Mindful breaths provide
>>>> arithmetic enough.

40-6

> If a breath inhaled
>> unawares is a poison-tipped blade,
>>> why keep being impaled
>>>> on such a sword?

1511-9

> Were you aware of your inner Joseph
>> your every breath would carry
>>> his shirt's fragrance.

855-4

> Breath requires life-long vigilance:
>> an excuse-laden breeze has thrown
>>> my guttering candle under siege.

1936-7

> Why should the awakened rise
>> from a meditative trance
>>> when angelic sprites dance
>>>> in every breath-filled purlieu?

On The Road

1743-1

> From within its oyster shell
>> a pearl can't very well
>>> open its eye. Travel
>>>> unravels the visionary knot.

2645-10

> This vale of bewilderment
>> merits checking out.
>>> Put oh for a compass's
>>>> steel-shod feet!

1507-3

> To the pilgrim with fire in his soles
>> each plant on the trail
>>> glows with a beckoning light.

1186-6

> The myopic
> misconceive
> pirate
> and pilot.
> The clear-sighted
> know their very next

step
may pitch
into a pit.

488-6

Heedless of dips and rises
 I fasten eyes on my goal. The ground
  levels once I stop
   querying each step.

813-4

A remote goal motivates the traveler.
 Too quick a trip makes people lazy.

12-2

Scurrying from site to site
 raises little but dust.
  Attainment invites
   a more inward thrust.

706-2

Pity the traveler who attains his goal.
 What's a stagnant pool
  but tarnished glass?

775-11

Not easy to convince the naive
 of the sights derived
  once sight-seeing ceases.

1176-6

No one comes by the Signless
 following road signs.
  The Truth-seeker requires
   neither the Ka'ba nor the fire
    temple.

1997-2

> The least whiff of self keeps the seeker
> roadbound. Where this load
> tumbles from your shoulders
> there's your spot.

952-3

> Other than Love's threshold
> what destination can there be?
> Who, from such a portal,
> would embark for Mecca?

681-1

> Weaklings bemoan the hazards of the Quest.
> Love may be a pain
> but it alleviates many another.

1121-6

> Like a black
> adder
> tarmac
> attacks
> those who stray.
> I walk
> where no footprints
> can distract.

775-8

> To retrace a swift-moving mystic's
> footprints would be like
> mapping the meanderings
> of an ocean stream.

377-4

> Only now at my road-end
> is my journey underway. My destiny
> has outpaced my road.

A Lap Full of Stones

1852-7

We walk, eyes fixed on the ground,
unaware how each star
in the cosmos charts
our least stride.

1515-2

How can you attain the gist
of the Truth if you believe the heavens
rotate serendipitously?

732-7

To my jaundiced eye, our firmament's
gem-like stars mask
a lap full of stones.

1113-7

Can it be that the firmament
out of pity canopies the earth?
Why else would our barren table
merit such raiment?

681-3

To ascribe a man's crimes to his stars
is like accusing the sonnambulist
of being a burglar.

476-5

Every night the stars snip
another thread from my allotted skein.
Every day my sieve-
like holes tighten.

820-9

> I'll be heading soon to a peak
> > in the Great Void where no planets
> > > will plague me.

1079-13

> How, from within a bubble, may a wave
> > extend its limpid arc?
> Clear out of the cosmos, Saeb,
> > if you truly desire unfettered latitude.

My Life

2351-7

> Try to gauge my life story.
> > I'm still hidden
> > > in a hundred thousand mirrors.

2488-13

> Though my pen raised poetry's profile
> > what I sought of a life
> > > expired in its pursuit.

2639-6

> A vast scatter of gems
> > I bequeathed to mankind;
> > > but no candle,
> > > > other than an owl's eyes
> > > > > consecrates my ruins.

2618-2

> Little left but a sigh:
> > a thousand foes;
> > > a single arrow.

photo from along old Route 66 by Karen Koshgarian

John Brandi

North on Hwy 84

Crash, he called himself
extending a high-five, numbers on his
knuckles, dagger in his palm. He fidgeted
trying to fasten his seat belt, then threw it off
with a thrust of exaggerated anger.

Went to see my ex, man she looks
dumpier than hell —shacked up with another
when they sent me up, anyhow I'm out now
looking for something to do.

Drove him ninety miles
from where I picked him up, the road straight
and dark, until we got to the mountains
where we stopped at a 7/11
because he wanted cigarettes.

We both got out
but I had to tell him this was as far
as I wanted company. Got some things
to think about, I said—

The look he gave me
sent shivers up my spine.
Got back in, drove the last sixty miles
to Durango, my high beams on
for the rest of the ride.

Renee Gregorio

Do

And if there were a way
what would it look like?

scent of laurel
fragrance of evergreen
the bouquet he gave to me,
saying each flower was chosen
"with opening in mind."

not past or future but here, now
feeling this earth-blanket of wildflower

and the backdrop of death
best friend's mother
best friend's husband
best friend
lover gone these 20 years
this particular unhinging
a dislocation
like when I take the feeder away
how the hummingbirds
still full of desire and hunger
hover around the space it once occupied

one fall equinox
in the sweep and dive and depth of mountain
at the summit near the empty lake
I asked the mountain what my name is

the altitude took my breath away
but I kept climbing
and the mountain's only answer —
a deepening silence

once I saw a boy scratch the back of his head
with a sickle as he walked down the dirt road

once I saw a son with a crooked nose
knew he'd become a man with a crooked nose

once in a blue lit afternoon
in a city I love but don't live in
the gulls came all at once, swooping
hard and fast and together
toward all of us lying on the grass
and it seemed it had to have been choreographed
but, if so, by whom
and I thought: love is that way
a swooping thing on its way somewhere else
but timing together

in some places women don't like to wear shoes
because they can't feel their feet on the earth

if I left my heart in Bubaneshwar [1]
then what's the heart that's still here with me?

I learn to be afraid and act anyway

—how to see a fossil in a rock
then see them everywhere

—how to hold the hand of absence
and to call, even him, beloved

I learn what's beyond betrayal is still practice
what's beyond the gate, another arrival

I learn to let a cold shower make me strong

—that sometimes when I turn my head
there is a tiny room bursting with candlelight

from a thousand butter lamps

I learn how to dance to Chuck Berry with a tight sacrum
—how to weave through the dark and the light
—how to talk to the water at Soberanes Point [2]
—how to make crazy love in the creaking bed
—how even when the fog is thick, the lighthouse beam is clear.

---

[1] Bubaneshwar=Capital city of the Indian state of Orissa (Odisha).
[2] Soberanes Canyon (and Rocky Ridge)=A redwood canyon with hiking trails in Garrapata State Park on the Central California coast.

E. A. "Tony" Mares

Driving with Vered and Juana *La Loca* in Mexico

We're rolling along in the VW bus,
my daughter Vered,
Juana *la Loca** and me, across
the Sierra Madre Occidental.
Goodbye, Morelia, and on we go
through drizzle and fog
on the black mirror road
reflecting sunlight glitter
off the slippery surface.

Down below, we see the skeletons
of wrecked cars, busses, trucks
that tumbled off the tight turns
and came to rest like the bones
of ancient animals on the steep cliffs.

"I need candles to pray," says
Crazy Juana. "Pray is okay.
No candles," I shout over the road noise.
"If I don't light candles, I'll freak out."
"Freak out. That's okay." Vered
tries to distract Juana *la Loca*
as I try to keep the VW on the road.
"Remember we're loaded with *aditivo*,"
"If you light candles, we'll go off
like a bomb," says Vered.

You could smell the fuel additive
for cars in a low octane country.
It works. Juana calms down.
After Guadalajara, after Mazatlán,
after Culiacán, after Nogales,
we're back in the USA. Vered
grows up. Juana disappears.

Now I think of Juana. Those trips.
Her prayers and her candles.
I could use them now. So could Mexico.

G. L. Brower

Everywhere No One Expected to Find You

For my mother, Freeda C. Brower (4/17/1917–4/23/2008)

I assumed a fetal position inside my grief
when I found out the womb that once held me
took your life.

Though the surgeon slit the throat of the invader,
you couldn't float in the small lake of air
where lungs paddled shallow.
Trauma slowly drowned your small body.

In the ICU, you wore the gladiator mask
for the forces of oxygen
to fight in the arena of your bed,
while on the walls I imagined your landscapes, animals, birds,
pictures from before arthritis grabbed brushes from your hands,
and I heard you sing, your voice from decades past,
in my memory's ear
in small towns and churches that disappeared
in the twilight of your voice.

Years after your infant sister died before you
you lost your childhood,
after a stranger with a strange name strangled your legs,
after your parents went bankrupt trying to move
the immovable paralysis from your body,
after doctors said you could never do what you later did,
some believing you couldn't continue your family's genealogy,–
cause of your later fascination with the generational Who's Who–
in waning fortunes of a waning family.

When I was born, child of our abandonment by the man
who got cold feet after the wedding,
after he avoided the WWII Draft by marrying you,
they told you I would die,

a boat too small in the amniotic ocean–that somehow reached
      shore,
living proof of your maternal ability for doubters,
just as wooden sticks propped much of your walk through life,
allowed mobility, and later work,
driving a car with hand brake and special pedal,
let everyone know you were human after all.

You saved your anger for those who looked at you with cheap
      pity.

When you and my real father,
the second, an orphan, who did what the first wouldn't,
decided to marry,
you came to ask me, the child between you,
what I thought,
surprised when I asked for the when of what you wanted.

And so, two outsiders, orphan and polio victim,
joined unlikely, till death did they part,
sixty-one years down the dance floor.

When your father/my grandfather died,
when your mother/my grandmother died,
when your daughter-in-law/my wife died,
when her parents/ my in-laws died,
when your friends/ my friends died,
when your unknown sister/ my unknown aunt died,
when your husband/ my step-and-only father died,
when it seemed the world was a small clearing in a forest of
      death
where we tried to prepare life like a meal over a fire made of fear,
traveling between villages named Alpha and Omega
along paths in the palms of our hands,
it seemed our tears became grains of sand

in an hourglass that fell to the ground
breaking years into days, hours into minutes, jagged pieces of
        time,
we tried to restore with the glue of memory.

You moved your rowboat though life with crutches as oars,
arriving in unknown places,
everywhere no one expected to find you,
said if you got to heaven
you would ask for legs not wings
because you loved to watch dancers
glide on the slide of sound.

If only you could dance away pain,
the dark, indelible ink of sadness
that now sketches your empty portrait,
if only I could see you dance beyond the whirl in my heart,
see you swing to the Blue Danube with my father,
if only crutches could dance,
if only I could let go of your hand,
see you two-step and twirl
everywhere
no one
expected
to find you.

Cuba's Nancy Morejón:
A Poet Who Lives In Her Poems
by G. L. Brower

One of Cuba's most well known, well-published, and widely-traveled poets today is Nancy Morejón, whose reputation grows constantly, and whose work has been translated into several languages. She has picked up the mantle of her mentor, the island nation's Poet Laureate for many years, Nicolás Guillén (1902-1989). Both are Afro-Cuban and bring that important cultural aspect into their work but don't write exclusively on topics from that background. Morejón says she is a tripartite person: a woman, of African background, and a Cuban, and none of these three elements can be separated from each other. (See her interview with NYC poet/novelist Sapphire in a 2011 interview online in *Bomb Magazine*.) Morejón has won Cuba's National Prize for Literature (2000) and the Critic's Prize (1986), has published two books on Guillén,* and was the first Afro-Cuban woman to graduate from the University of Havana's Faculty of the Arts (her degree is in French and Caribbean literatures). Born in 1944 to working class parents in Havana, she eventually became the President of UNEAC (the Cuban Writers and Artist Union) and the Editor of *Union*, its literary journal. She has also translated noted writers into Spanish from both French and English, including such Caribbean poets as Aimé Césaire and Rene Depestre.

Two of her most famous poems are *Mujer Negra* (Black Woman) and *Amo a mi Amo* (I love my Master), the first attacking slavery with the story of a woman brought over on a slave-ship, the second about the plight of the slave once in the western hemisphere.

From the first poem:

> I still smell the foam of the sea they made me cross.
> The night, I can't remember.
> The ocean itself couldn't remember it.
> But I can't forget the first gull I saw in the distance.
> The clouds, high, like innocent witnesses.
> Perhaps I haven't forgotten my lost coast,
> nor my ancestral language.
> They left me here and here I've lived.
> And because I worked like an animal,
> here I came to be born.
>
> I rebelled. (....)
>
> I walked. (....)
>
> This is the land where I suffered
> dust in my mouth and the lash.
> I rode the length of all its rivers.
> Under its sun I planted seeds, brought in the crops,
> but never ate those harvests.
> A slave barracks was my house,
> built with stones I hauled. (....)

Morejón has published some 18 books of poetry (not counting the translations) and has toured the Europe, Latin America, and the U.S., reading her work. In the latter, she lectured at Wellesley College and the University of Missouri-Columbia, where a 2-day symposium on her work was held in 1995. (The papers were published in a special issue of the *Afro-Hispanic Review*.) Howard University Press published a collection of critical essays on Morejón's poetry in 1999, *Singular like a Bird: The Art of Nancy Morejón*, edited by Dr. Miriam DaCosta-Willis. In 2005, an anthology of her poetry was published, *Richard brought his flute*, edited by the noted Uruguayan poet Mario Benedetti (now deceased). There are three books of English translations of her work (none of which have I seen): *Mirar Adentro: Looking within: Selected Poems, 1954-2000* (Wayne State University Press, 2002, edited by Juanamaría Cordares-Cook); *Where the Island Sleeps like a Wing* (San Francisco, Black Scholar Press, 1985, ed. and translated by Kathleen Weaver); *With Eyes and Soul: Images of Cuba* (White Pine Press, 2004, ed. and translation by Pamela Carmell and David Frye).

---

* Her two books on Nicolás Guillén are *Nación y Mestizaje en Nicolás Guillén* (1982), and a compilation of texts about Guillén (1974). I'm not aware they have been translated into English.
Translations of all poems by GLB.

La Noche Del Moncada

La noche era más linda, era como algo
que merecía verse toda la vida,
y a lo mejor que no veríamos más.
–Haydée Santamaría

Pasaron treinta años.
Como pasan los cometas en el espacio.
Pasaron treinta noches exactas
y aquella noche fue más noche
porque, tal vez, sería la última
o la primera noche de una época estrenada.
Los ojos de Abel pudieron contemplarla todavía.
Hasta hoy llega el perfume
de la noche silvestre, duradera,
entre las hierbas de la granjita Siboney
y el brillo de los fusiles navegando en el pozo del patio.

Hasta hoy se escuchan los disparos
que median entre aquella noche grande
donde unos jóvenes comieron, cocinaron, cantaron
y nos hicieron una noche más dulce.
Pasaron treinta años, treinta noches del trópico
y pensar que esta noche yo vivo el privilegio
de contemplar otra noche tan linda,
sin más ni menos luna, sin más ni menos ansias,
otra noche tan grande,
que vive en el aliento de la libertad
mientras respiro ésta, aquella noche,
que merecía verse toda la vida.

Moncada Night [1]

"The night was beautiful, it was like something
that was worth seeing all your life
and that we likely won't see again."
—Haydée Santamaría [2]

Thirty years passed.
Like comets pass in outer space.
Thirty exact nights passed
and that night was more nightly
because, perhaps, it will be the last
or the first night of an inaugural epoch.
Abel's eye could still contemplate it.[3]
The lasting perfume of that
wild night, arrives up to today,
in the grains of the little Siboney farm [4]
and the shine on the rifles navigating around the patio well.

Even today the gunshots can be heard
that gauge that big night
where some youths cooked, ate, sang
and made a very sweet night.
Thirty years passed, thirty tropical nights
and to think that tonight I live the privilege
of contemplating another beautiful evening
without much moon, much anxiety,
another immense night
that lives in the breath of liberty
while I breathe this one, that very night,
that merits being seen all my life.

-----

1 Moncada=On July 26, 1953, Fidel Castro and a group of 140 cohorts attacked the Moncada Barracks of the Cuban dictator Batista's army, in Santiago de Cuba. The attack was a failure, with many imprisoned attackers, but it was said this effort "was the small engine that ignited the big engine of the Revolution" later, which was successful in 1959.

2 Haydée Santamaría (1923-1980) was a guerrilla with Fidel, a part of the attacking group on the Moncada Barracks. Upon her release from jail, after the failed attack, she founded the July 26 Movement and joined Castro and his guerrillas in the Sierra Maestra Mountains. After the triumph of the Revolution, she founded the main arts organization in Cuba, *Casa de Las Américas*.

3 This line refers to Abel Santamaría (1923-1953), brother of Haydée, who was also imprisoned after the failure of the attack on the Moncada Barracks. Batista's jailers tore out one of his eyes (and threatened to do the same to the other) because he refused to talk. They took the one eye to Haydée, who supposedly said: "If you tore out an eye and he didn't talk, neither will I."

4 Siboney=A town in eastern Cuba, named for an extinct Indian tribe, which engendered a famous 1929 song by Ernesto Lecuona. Some of the Moncada attackers stayed at a small farm in the town the night before the attack.

Movimiento Perpetuo

Una mañana de pronto es una noche.
La madera del bosque es de pronto una hoja de papel.
El arroyuelo entre los valles es poco a poco
el océano profundo y azulado.
Una fragua de fuego es mañana, de noche,
una brillante fuente de cristal.

Sobre cualquier desierto grávido
sólo encuentras arenas
únicamente removidas
por el viento ligero de los aires.

¿Quién te asegura que no llegará un día
el próspero aguacero?
Tanto se mueven las cosas a tu alrededor.
Hasta tu país cambió. Lo has cambiado tú misma.
No es ya la Isla en el Golfo
reverberando entre las cañas
sino reverberando entre fusiles.
El Tiburón, con su espantosa lágrima,
fue arponeado para siempre en tu Isla
y la Sardina acude al funeral.

La tierra de la tembladera
no es sólo barro contrahecho
sino que continúa su curso,
devoradora de todo lo animado.

Ayer, a pleno sol, el hueso de la muerta
engendró yerbabuena.
Para su ensoñación mejor,
el buey apacentado
lame el estiércol de los gorriones.

Qué fría la luna.
Qué sol fosforescente.

Y el alma, ¿cambiará?
Has de cambiarla tú.
¿Será inhóspito el tránsito?
¿Habrá de ser palpable,
sin una gota de violencia?
Mientras seas la de hoy
siendo con creces la de ayer,
serás la de mañana.
Serás la misma y serás siempre,
al mismo tiempo, otra,
la que vive y que muere
para vivir así.

_____

(De *Peñalver 51*, 2010)

Perpetual Motion

A morning is quickly night.
Forest wood is quickly a piece of paper.
The rivulet between valleys little by little is
the deep blue sea.
A fiery forge is morning, by night,
a shiny crystal fountain.

Over any heavy desert
you only find sands
uniquely moved around
by a light wind.

Who assures you that a propitious shower
won't arrive one day?
So much do things move around you.
Even your country changed. You changed it yourself.
It's not just an island in the Gulf
reverberating among strands of sugarcane
but among stands of rifles.
The Shark, with its scary tear,[1]
was harpooned forever on your Island
and the Sardine attends the funeral.

The quaking earth
isn't only deformed mud
but it continues its course,
devourer of everything animated.

Yesterday, in full sun, the bone of the dead woman
generated mint.
To better its illusion,
the peaceful oxen
licks the dung of sparrows.

How cold the Moon.
What phosphorescent sun.
And the Soul, will it change?
You have to change it yourself.
Will its passage be difficult?
Will it be palpable,
without a drop of violence?
While being today's
being amply yesterday's,
you will be tomorrow's.
You will be the same and always will be,
at the same time, another,
the one that lives and dies
in order to live so.

(From: *Peñalver 51*, 2010)

1 The references to "The Shark and the Sardines" is to the title of a famous book by Juan José Arévalo (1904-1990), President of Guatemala titled *Fable of the Shark and the Sardines* (1956). The book was popular and influential for at least 20 years, especially throughout Latin America. The basic metaphor was that the U.S. (the Shark) dominated the smaller Central American and Caribbean nations (the Sardines).

Qana

Oh dios si existes

No he dudado de tu existencia

Esa pregunta,
lanzada al vórtice de los vacíos,
es un gorrión con las alas quemadas;
como una gruta sorda
por donde caminamos, sin rumbo,
hasta que el cuerpecito ensangrentado
de una niña inocente
impide el paso

Luego,
hay un sonido atronador que nos lleva
hasta un letrero que dice QANA

Oh dios si existes

Cómo podrías explicar
tanto sadismo, tanta crueldad, tanta aberración

Es alucinante ver la sangre de una niña brotar

La sangre de una niña yerta, yerta, yerta
Su mirada, agua de alondras, yerta

Brota la sangre
de su cabeza y de sus piernecitas

Oh dios de todos los días

Cualquiera que fuese tu nombre o tu pasado o tu origen;
dondequiera que hayas reinado o sufrido;
dondequiera que te hayan rendido culto

Ven a calmarla
Ven a mitigar su dolor y mi espanto
Ven y acúnala en tus brazos,
Ven en su auxilio porque mis lágrimas no pueden hacer
nada,
     ni mis ruegos, ni mis versos inciertos.

Haz posible la cordura entre los hombres y sus familias,
entre las mujeres y sus familias,
entre las niñas y los niños y sus familias
desencontradas o encontradas
de todo el orbe
y que los culpables de estos crímenes paguen por ellos.

Cana

Oh god if you exist

I haven't doubted your existence

This question,
thrown into the vortex of the void,
is a sparrow with burned wings;
like a quiet cavern
we walk through, directionless,
till the bloody body
of an innocent little girl
impedes passage.

Then,
there is a thundering sound that takes us
to a sign that says CANA [1]

Oh god is you exist

How can you explain
so much sadism, cruelty, mania

It's hallucinatory to see blood gush from a little girl
the blood of a motionless, stiff, rigid little girl
her look, water of larks, motionless

Blood gushes
from her head and little legs

oh god of all our days

Whatever your name or past or origin might be;
wherever you might have ruled or suffered;
wherever they might have worshipped you

come to calm her
come to mitigate her pain and my horror
come and take her in your arms,
come to her aid because my tears can't do
anything,
        my pleas, nor my uncertain verses.

Make possible cordiality between men and their families,
between women and their families,
between girls and boys and their families
found or not
all over the world
and that those guilty of these crimes pay for them.

---

1 Cana/Qana=A southern Lebanese village attacked twice by the Israeli
Air Force in 1996, when a UN facility full of refugees was hit, with
many children killed; and then again in 2006 in a war between Israel
and Hesbollah, also with many children killed.

Michael C. Ford

From Flatbush to George Bush

*For Harry Northrup, who's seen more Dodger games
in Brooklyn & LA than anyone could possible imagine*

INTRODUCTION
*My feeling was that much of what happened to pro-baseball is
metaphorically aligned with the evolution of the U.S. Government.
There's been an obvious negative evolution between the Eisenhower
years, when the Dodgers were playing in Brooklyn, to when they
migrated to the Coliseum in Los Angeles. I believe that the corruption
of our political system along with the gradual corporate rip-off of major
league baseball are very easily aligned. I know they used to refer to
Brooklyn as Flatbush, so when it came time to think about a title for this
baseball narrative/poem, the imp of the perverse perched on my shoulder
and tweaked my imagination. I just couldn't help thinking of that
borough and the G.W. Bush League regime. –MCF*

I genuflect in front of soft altars supporting the innocence &
optimism of those Brooklyn days, somehow turning, with the
turning of the years, into the hard, cold control of corporate
monopoly & our only rebellion is a memory of Bronx cheers
spouted into the Summertime fidelity for the American sport of
baseball.

I genuflect in front of the time when trolley cars rattled down
roads in Brooklyn & the hometown team was called the *Trolley
Dodgers.*

I genuflect in front of the Red Car[1] that shuttled along a network
of LA inner-city streets taking us to where we could still be
enamored by ecstatic round-trippers, by Steve Bilko.[2]

I genuflect in front of *Pacific Electric* roads being paved over to
pave the way for major league ball to go West, because
streetcar transit was cutting into General Motors and Goodyear
Tires & Standard Oil annuities: so they ripped the rails outta
Brooklyn: the same way they ripped apart the struts

supporting that wooden Cathedral ballpark & there are those
who still pray to the ghosts of Ebbets Field.

I genuflect in front of the memory of a choir-loft grandstand,
where the hullabaloo belle of the bleachers Hilda Chester [3] would
reside: her cowbell constantly clanging in Van Gogh's other ear.

I genuflect in front of the sacristy of the bullpen progeny of
Preacher Roe, Carl Erskine, Clem Labine, Larry Sherry, Tommy
John, Johnny Podres, Koufax, Drysdale, Hersheiser, Ron
Perranoski, Fernando Valenzuela, Don Newcombe: even the
fated Ralph Branca.

I genuflect in front of the continuity of iconic follow-through
swings by Dixie Walker, Frenchy Bordagaray, Furillo, Snider,
Campanella, Johnny Roseboro, Gene Hermanski,
Pete Reiser, Pee Wee Reese, George "Shotgun" Shuba,
Lou Johnson, Kirk Gibson, Gil Hodges & Wally Moon.

I genuflect in front of the 1955 World Series: Jackie Robinson
robbing home plate signifying yet another reminder that
Branch Rickey broke up the double plays of intolerant repression.

I genuflect in front of the aggressive wrecking-ball that battered
into Chavez Ravine while we witnessed thru smog eyes the
construction of Dodger Stadium like a bullring *corrida* against
the old days, against the gold days; the civil wars between
expendable Chicanos & real estate profiteering: exactly the
same way endless political controversy batters apart what's left
of our disabled democracy.

I genuflect in front of Walter O'Malley's life raft floating farther &
farther away from the sinking boat of Bum's Paradise &
shipwrecking on the jagged reefs of expansion-team conspiracy.

I genuflect in front of this pastoral game played in the middle of a malaise of urban congestion: the Bum Saints of Flatbush arrive in LA to be compromised by Ivy League nerds with their trades, their trade-offs, free *agentry* & organized disloyalties.

I genuflect in front of these murderous intrusions into a circumference of terrorized nations that revere declarations of patriotic revenge: that no matter where your political loyalties lie, since the Dodgers moved to LA, there's been a lotta rough stuff goin' on: not that our existing executive wing of government hasn't been any more morally responsible than any other during the last 50 years: I mean, think about it for a minute!

I genuflect in front of the time when Dwight David Eisenhower {leaving his term as President} issued a warning to beware of the industrial military corporate complex & nobody listened: opening the door to the Kennedy/Johnson architects of the Vietnam War for the profit machine & now the US government & American military have the war they always wanted: the war that will have no end.

I genuflect in front of the knowledge that Shakespeare would never have hung up his spikes, if he knew, now, how much we needed a redeeming rhymed couplet. If Willie S. could lather up his glove & come back to write a final play to turn us away from our terrors, I'm sure he would set it in Flatbush & it would probably be called: **A Tragedy of Errors**.

―――――

1 The Red Cars were part of the consolidated Pacific Electric urban transportation system in Los Angeles (1897-1950). Not only in LA but all across the nation, large cities had their electric trolley car and bus systems that took care of their transport needs but in the 1950s without consulting citizens and voters, city and county politicians and governments destroyed their own systems and bought gas-guzzling buses at the behest of bus companies/manufacturers, gas/oil companies (read Detroit). A few cities kept their old systems-such as New Orleans. Later, it turned out that city/county politicians had been secretly bribed to do this. It was expensive to rip out the rails and then the buses used expensive gas rather than cheaper electricity, which meant they had to charge riders more, which meant the system was less profitable, worse for consumers.

2 Steve Bilko (1928-1978) was a famous player in the 1950s & 1960s for the Los Angeles Angels in the Pacific Coast League, then in the American League.

3 The "Queen of the Bleachers," Hilda Chester, for more than 30 years, became famous as the most fanatic fan in baseball history, specifically for the Brooklyn Dodgers, beginning in the 1920s. She became known as "Howling Hilda" and was given free passes to the games, later known for her use of a cowbell to foster fan enthusiasm.

4 This poem was commissioned by the LA Mayor's Department of Cultural Affairs in collaboration with the Baseball Reliquary, which is a floating museum installing itinerant exhibitions of relics identifying with the history of American baseball. The director of the Reliquary, Terry Cannon, asked MCF to write something on the topic of moving the Dodgers to LA. to which the poet said: "Terry, I'm not even a New Yorker, but I realize the fact that to a lot of people, the bulldozing of Ebbets Field wasn't a reason to celebrate, it was a reason to have a funeral." MCF read this poem at the event but it was controversial because of the political comments.

This poem reminds me -to a certain extent- of the Ed Dorn poem titled "The World Box-Score Cup of 1966" which focused on soccer rather than baseball but also had elements of politics mixed with a game, but with a political announcer (the poet) describing the game between the "Haves" and the "Have-nots." See: Ed Dorn, *The Collected Poems, 1956-1974* (Bolinas, Four Seasons, 1975), pp. 162-178.

Joan Logghe

The Last Streetcar

*for Gerald Stern**

In the last dream of streetcars it was yellow
and fast, tracks close to the curb so you couldn't pass
but I did. I think it was his streetcar and I wonder
is he well, and is she there watching him grow
even more beautiful and impossible as he runs down? Gold
watch. Yellow Streetcar. Carefully shaving the throat.

Did he know Ubby Cohen, the most reprobate
of the Jewish men of Pittsburgh, the bad influence
with his shikse wife? And my father, did they ever cross paths,
drink in the same bar? Did they pass
on Northumberland Street with French poems
in his heart and in my father's, the clothing store?

I grew up with wool swatches to play with, white on white shirts,
and taking inventory. Why was he my teacher for only ten days
and my father my father beyond death?
Why was my father carrying my one poem in his wallet
until he died? Was he buried on Blackamore Street
with my one poem? Did he ever meet a man

twenty years his junior crooning in the Hill District?
Did they agree Dean Martin was better than Sinatra?
Did my father see a man dancing and wonder
what the women saw in him? Did they ever squeeze
by on the narrow stairway up to the speakeasy on Walnut
that was called The Hollywood Social Club?

Or did my brother's friend, Toby, wildest of those guys
ever have a law case defending poetry? Did he post
bail for an illicit poem? In the last dream of streetcars I asked no
questions. Felt the physical thrust and rush of yellow yellow
yellow on Ellsworth Avenue, bright as a taxi,
on this week of my high school reunion

which I attended the only way I could, which is in dreams
and inquisition. Where is my dream father now?
My dear teacher, how is his mind? And the next generation who
never set foot in a streetcar, how can they stand swaying, and
how can they bear the French poets? Who will carry Rimbaud?
Who holds out a hand for Baudelaire?

Where will my old books sail in my wake? What becomes
of erudition after the streetcars are gone?

------

* Gerald Stern (b. 1925) is a well known poet born in Pittsburgh, Pa.,
like the author of this poem. Stern is the author of some 20 books of po-
etry and has taught at numerous universities: Iowa Writers Workshop,
New England College, Temple University, Drew University, University
of Alabama, Washington University, Columbia, Bucknell Universities,
and others. He was the Poet Laureate of New Jersey (2002-2002), won
the National Book Award for Poetry (1998), and one of his books was a
finalist for the Pulitzer Prize in 1991.

photo from along old Route 66 by Karen Koshgarian

THE DUENDE POETRY SERIES
OF PLACITAS, NEW MEXICO
invites you to attend our readings four times per year
(March, June, September & one floating date)
always at 3pm on a Sunday at
Anasazi Fields Winery, Placitas, New Mexico.

For current schedule: www.anasazifieldswinery.com/events

Since 2004, our readers have included:

Dorothy Alexander
Cathy Arellano
Maisha Baton
Hakim Bellamy
Sherwin Bitsui
Rich Boucher
John Brandi
Gary L. Brower
Nathan Brown
J.B. Bryan
Bobby Byrd
Lauren Camp
Álvaro Cardona-Hine
Albino Carrillo
Debbie Coy
Wayne Crawford
Doris Fields
Jim Fish
Damien Flores
Michael C. Ford
Anne Valley Fox
Gene Frumkin
Lisa Gill
Gary Mex Glazner
Renny Golden
Larry Goodell
Art Goodtimes
John Orne Green
Renee Gregorio

Donald Gurevich
Joy Harjo (& her band)
Dale Harris
Michelle Holland
Bruce Holsapple
Stefan Hyner
Zachary Kluckman
Jim Koller
Joanne Kyger
Enrique LaMadrid
Donald Levering
Maria Leyba
Joan Logghe
Jessica Helen Lopez
Suzanne Lummis
John Macker
Amalio Madueño
E.A. "Tony" Mares
Howard McCord
Mary McGinnis
James McGrath
Don McIver
Karen McKinnon
Anne McNaughton
Todd Moore
Sawnie Morris
Carol Moscrip
Jules Nyquist
Mary Oishi

Simon Ortiz with
    Sara Marie &
    Rainy Dawn Ortiz
Bill Pearlman
Janine Pommy-Vega
    with J'Zaam
Peter Rabbit
Margaret Randall
Mitch Rayes
John Roche
Leo Romero
Levi Romero
Georgia Santa Maria
Andrea Serrano
Cirrelda Snyder-Bryan
Joe Somoza
Marilyn Stablein
Luci Tapahonso
Dick Thomas
John Tritica
Richard Vargas
Mark Weber
Lawrence Welsh
Heloise Wilson
Jason L. Yurcic

CONTRIBUTORS

Hakim Bellamy: Inaugural Poet Laureate of Albuquerque, New Mexico (2012-2014); Founder and CEO of Beyond Poetry LLC. He was the featured poet in *MR* v4#3 Winter 2013-14. www.hakimbe.com and www.beyondpoetryink.com

John Brandi: Associated with the Post-Beat Generation of poets and originally from southern California, he has lived in New Mexico for many years in the El Rito area. A world traveler who likes to use travel as inspiration for poetry, he published Tooth of Time Press for many years. He has published eight books of poetry, seven of haiku/haibun, five books of stories, and some translations. He is also a visual artist, and was awarded an NEA Fellowship as well as a Witter Bynner Foundation translation grant.

G. L. Brower has taught at various universities, has published three volumes of poetry and two CDs in the last five years. He is one of the directors of the Duende Poetry Series of Placitas, NM. Recent publications include *The Wanekia & Other Poems* and *In Paradise, People Will Become Music* (both poetry CDs), and *Leaving Cairo, As If It Were A Dream* (a collaboration of poetry with photos by J. M. Gay, Jr., and a CD).

Christine Eber lives in Las Cruces, New Mexico. She is an anthropologist who works with Maya women and their families in highland Chiapas, Mexico. Since retiring from teaching at New Mexico State University she has been writing poetry. She is co-founder of Weaving for Justice, an organization that assists weavers in Chiapas to sell their weavings so they are not forced to migrate. Her poems have been published in *Adobe Walls* and *Anthropology and Humanism.*

Leon Felipe (1884-1968) was a major Spanish poet associated with the famous Generation of 1927 (which included Lorca, Alberti, Salinas, etc.) and considered one of the best in Spanish poetry. Trained as a pharmacist, he practiced his profession because of the wishes of his family but soon went over to poetry. He published some 17 books of poetry, collected in his *Poesías Completas* (Mexico, 1963). He translated Whitman into Spanish and in turn some of his work was called "Whitmanesque." He was a leader in the large Spanish exile community in Mexico.

Michael C. Ford is one of the most well-known poets in the Los Angeles area. His first public reading was at a fundraiser for Norman Mailer's run for New York City mayor (1969), where he read with Jack Hirschman, Michael McClure and The Doors' Jim Morrison. In the late 1970s, he was a co-editor of *The Sunset Palms Hotel*, a literary magazine. Ford is a teacher, critic, playwright, and recording artist who has published 20 books of poetry. These include the Pulitzer Prize nominated *Emergency Exits* (Selected Poems, 1970-95); *Nursery Rhyme Assassin* (2000); *To Kiss the Blood Off Our Hands* (2007); *The Marilyn Monroe Concerto* (2008); and *The Demented Chauffeur & Other Mysteries* (2009). He has also been involved in collaborative recordings with The Doors' drummer John

Densmore and keyboardist/pianist Ray Manzarek as well as with trombonist Julian Priester. Ford's debut spoken word recording, *Language Commando* (1986), was nominated for a Grammy.

Larry Goodell was born in 1935 in Roswell, New Mexico, and has lived in Placitas since 1963. He is known for extending poetry into its ceremonial roots – performance, masks, costume, lighting, song, scene with cloth or painted backdrops when appropriate. Although tagged as a performance poet since the early 60's, he loves the printed page and founded duende press in '64. His writing comes from the myth of local inspiration, often from organic gardening and love for New Mexico. He is a risk-taker in language who avoids revision, considering the handwritten original as precedent. His work is often satirical and seriously funny. Books: *Cycles* (1966, duende press), *Firecracker Soup* (1990, Cinco Puntos Press), *Here on Earth* (1996, La Alameda Press). He's one of the directors of the Duende Poetry Series of Placitas. See http://about.me/larrygoodell for interviews, articles, numerous poems, plays, songs, and a blog on 3-dimensional poetry.

Renee Gregorio has published many chapbooks plus these poetry collections: *The Skins Of Possible Lives* (1996), *The Storm That Tames Us* (1999), *Water Shed* (2004), and *Drenched* (2010). Recent publications include *Love And Death: Greatest Hits* (Tres Chicas Books, 2011), a tripartite anthology of work by poets Renee Gregorio, Joan Logghe and Miriam Sagan; and *Road To Cloud's House: A Chiapas Journal* (2009), with her husband, poet and painter John Brandi. Gregorio received grants for writing residencies at the Mabel Dodge Luhan House in Taos and at the Millay Colony for the Arts in New York state. She has also taught classes and workshops at New Mexico Military Institute, the Taos Institute, Harwood Art Center and at Little River Poetics. She was a visiting professor at Colorado College and taught at San Juan College. She holds an M.A. in creative writing from Antioch University (London) and is a third-degree black belt in the martial art of Aikido.

Kenneth P. Gurney lives in Albuquerque, NM, USA with his beloved Dianne. His latest collection of poems is *Curvature of a Fluid Spine*. To learn more visit kpgurney.me.

Dale Harris has made New Mexico her home since 1993 after Hurricane Andrew blew her out of Miami, Florida. Her varied art interests include Japanese style woodcut prints, pottery, poetry, and book making. She is associate editor of *Malpais Review*.

Karen Koshgarian is a retired California art educator, photographer and artist. She currently lives in Portland, Oregon on an extended creative art and photography sabbatical. For her 66th birthday year, she decided to drive Route 66 from Chicago to Santa Monica, putting the tires on as many of the oldest alignments as were still drivable. After 25 days of driving, and 10,000+ photographs, she created a self-published book called *Drive-by Shooting on Old Route 66 - A Camera's Point-of-View*. The ode to the road is more a poetic tome, rather than a tourist's guide.

Images are to be savored. Every photograph was literally taken either from the car, or by the car, on US Route 66. The book is currently available by contacting the artist at twokandoux@comcast.net.

Gayle Lauradunn's poems have been published in numerous journals and anthologies including *Queen of Swords Press, Sierra Club Books, Adobe Walls, Puerto del Sol, Zone 3, Tsunami,* and online. Some of her poems have been adapted and performed for the stage. She was the co-organizer for the first National Women's Poetry Festival, a 6-day event held at the University of Massachusetts, Amherst. She served on the Selection Committee for Albuquerque's first Poet Laureate.

Former NEA Fellow **Donald Levering's** 12th poetry book, *The Water Leveling With Us,* was published in 2014 by Red Mountain Press. He has worked as a groundskeeper, teacher on the Navajo reservation, and human services administrator. Featured in the Academy of American Poets Forum, the Ad Astra Poetry Project, and the Duende Series, he was a Finalist for the Janet B. McCabe Prize and the Jane Kenyon Award. A father of two children, he is married to the artist Jane Shoenfeld and lives in Santa Fe, New Mexico. Visit donaldlevering.com.

Carol Lewis, an Albuquerque poet, edited the poetry broadside "The Rag" for many years, and her poems have been published in innumerable journals.

Maria L. Leyba was born and raised in the Barelas neighborhood of Albuquerque's South Valley. She has spent her life listening to the beautiful voices of *mujeres* from Barelas *y* Mexico, the inspiration for many of her poems.

Lou Liberty, award winning poet, novelist, storyteller and historian, practices mindfulness, writing, and taiko drumming in Albuquerque's North Valley. She has received two National Endowment For Humanities fellowships resulting in limited edition poetry/photography anthologies. Lou has presented her work in numerous venues in New Mexico and throughout the U.S., Japan, Ireland, Great Britain, The Netherlands, Italy, Iceland, Canada and Turkey. The three poems in this issue of *Malpais Review* are from Lou's poetry collection, *Time Was and Time Was Not.*

Jane Lipman's first full-length poetry collection, *On the Back Porch of the Moon,* Black Swan Editions, 2012, won the 2013 New Mexico/Arizona Book Award for Poetry Book and a 2013 New Mexico Press Women's Award. She has published widely in journals and anthologies. Her chapbooks, *The Rapture of Tulips* and *White Crow's Secret Life,* were finalists for NM Book Awards in Poetry in 2009 and 2010, respectively.

Joan Logghe lives in northern New Mexico, is one of the publishers of Tres Chicas Press, and has just completed as Poet Laureate of Santa Fe. She has been the recipient of an NEA grant, Witter Bynner Poetry Foundation grant, a Mabel Dodge Luhan internship. She has taught in the Poetry-in-the-Schools Program, at UNM-Los Alamos, at Ghost Ranch in Abiquiu, and in Europe. Her books include: *Twenty Years in Bed with the Same Man; Blessed Resistance; Sofia;* and *Rice.*

Jessica Helen López is the current City of Albuquerque Poet Laureate. She has been on five city slam teams and is a two-time Women of the World Albuquerque champion. Founder of the collective *La Palabra* –The Word is a Woman, she is also the author of a Zia Book Award winning collection of poetry, *Always Messing With Them Boys* (West End Press, 2011) and the chapbook *Cunt. Bomb.* (Swimming With Elephants Publication, 2014). Jessica is a mama, teacher, feminist Xingona, Volunteer Coordinator for the upcoming 2015 Women of the World Poetry Slam tourney to be hosted in Albuquerque, and a wannabe gardener.

Suzanne Lummis is the director of The Los Angeles Poetry Festival which in fall of 2011 produced, together with Beyond Baroque, the 25-event, citywide series, "Night and the City: L.A. Noir in Poetry Fiction and Film". She has taught for many years through the UCLA Extension Writers' Program, regular workshops as well as special focus classes on the persona poem and poem noir. Her poems have appeared in noted literary magazines across the country, and in "New California Writing 2012" (Heyday Books), and the Knopf "Everyman's Library" anthologies, *Poems of the American West* and *Poems of Murder and Mayhem.*

Robin MacGowan: Santa Fe poet Robin MacGowan is the author of seven books of poetry and some volumes of translations. In the late 1980s, he lived in England and founded the transatlantic review MARGIN, which he edited till 1990. He also lived in France. He holds a BA from Harvard, and MA from Columbia and a Ph.D. from Yale in Comparative Literature. He has taught at the University of Washington and the University of California at Berkeley.

E.A. "Tony" Mares, Professor Emeritus from the University of New Mexico, is one of the state's most well-known writers. A journalist and historian as well as a poet, his works on Padre Martínez are important contributions to both history and literature. He was a part of the Chicano Literature renaissance centered in Embudo, NM. His latest books of poetry include *With the Eyes of a Raptor; Astonishing Light (Conversations I Never Had with Patrocinio Barela)* (UNM Press) and *Casi Toda la Música* (translations of poems by Spanish poet Ángel González).

Mary McGinnis has upcoming work in Lummox Press. Her full-length collection, *Listening For Cactus* is still available, along with *October Again.* She is working for herself now and loving life without going to the office.

Paula Miller is a retired psychotherapist living in Santa Fe and volunteering as a Court Appointed Special Advocate for abused children.

Gary Worth Moody's first collection of poems is *Hazards of Grace* (Red Mountain Press 2012). His second, *Occoquan*, (Red Mountain Press, 2015), depicts the struggles of women for emancipation and suffrage, in the environs of Virginia's infamous Occoquan Workhouse. A falconer, Gary lives in Santa Fe with the artist and writer, Oriana Rodman, two dogs and a red-tail hawk.

Nancy Morejón (b. 1944) is probably the most famous Cuban
269

poet today (along with Reina María Rodríguez), a Havana native who grew up in a working-class district of the city. She graduated from the University of Havana with a specialty in French and in Caribbean literature, the first black woman to do so in the Humanities. Fluent in French and English, she has published translations into Spanish from French. She has toured the U.S. more than once. In her early days as a burgeoning poet, she was mentored by Cuba's National Poet, Nicolas Guillén. The author of some 15 books of poetry, she has as well published works of literary criticism, including two on Guillén. There have been three books of her poetry published in translation into English.

Judy K Mosher, Ph.D. has called New Mexico home for almost 30 years. Besides writing poetry, she hikes Santa Fe's arroyos with her rescue golden retriever Jessie. She has poems published in *Adobe Walls, A Good Place to Stumble Upon, Noyo River Review, Santa Fe Literary Review,* and 200newmexicopoems.wordpress.com.

Sharon Niederman: Writer-photographer Sharon Niederman is author of 17 books of NM travel, cuisine, history, and culture, winner of the Lowell Thomas Travel Writing Award for *Signs & Shrines: Spiritual Journeys Across New Mexico* and a WILLA Award finalist for her novel *Return to Abo.* Her forthcoming book is *Enchanted Plate: New Mexico Farm to Table.* She lives in northeastern New Mexico.

Elizabeth O'Brien began writing poetry in a focused way since moving to Santa Fe seven years ago and has studied with New Mexico poets Miriam Sagan, Joan Logghe, and Jon Davis. She is a retired professor of American Literature who taught for twenty years at Drew University, Madison, N. J., and more recently at the College of Santa Fe, UNM, and IAIA. She is a member of three writing groups in Santa Fe: High Desert Poets, Escritores, and We Be Muses.

Mary Oishi is a New Mexico performance poet and KUNM-FM public radio personality. Although she had her first poem published nationally while in junior high school, *Spirit Birds They Told Me* (West End Press, 2011) is her first collection of poetry. She reads poetry at many venues in Albuquerque, and believes in the power of art to change the world. See: maryoishi.com or poetoishi.blogspot.com.

Marmika Paskiewicz lives and writes in Santa Fe, New Mexico. She has been published in several regional journals and is currently revising a chapbook and a memoir. Most recently she has studied with James Thomas Stevens at IAIA from whom she has learned a great deal.

Susan Paquet lives in Corrales, NM, with her husband, standard poodle and pet goats. She began writing poems and short stories a few years ago and has never had so much fun. Susan's writing has been published in various journals and anthologies in Texas and New Mexico.

Sylvia Ramos Cruz was born in Puerto Rico, grew up in New York City, and moved to New Mexico in 1990. She is a physician and surgeon who practices part-time. She loves words for their sounds and their ability to distill a personal experience into a shared humanity. She feels fortunate to be a member of an inspiring poetry writing group, the Albuquerque Word Weavers, and to participate in the vibrant Albuquerque writers' community.

Margaret Randall (b. New York 1936) has been writing poetry for 60 years. Her most recent collections are *My Town, As If The Empty Chair / Como Si La Silla Vacia, The Rhizome as a Field of Broken Bones, Where Do We Go From Here, Daughter of Lady Jaguar Shark,* and *About Little Charlie Lindbergh* (All From Wings Press, San Antonio, Texas), and *Ruins* (University of New Mexico Press). The second wave of feminism, in 1969, changed her life and has informed it ever since.

Denise Weaver Ross: Drawing on her experience as a graphic designer, printmaker and poet, Denise weaves layers of archetypes, myths, and personal experience into colorful, complex images. The work exhibits cubist strands in the use of simultaneous perspective, flattening, and fracturing of the image; surrealist strands similar to Chagall's dreamlike and thematic imagery; and strands from ancient art such as Egyptian and Byzantine iconography. Finally, it combines autobiographical, historical, cultural, and decorative elements into a unified tapestry.

Georgia Santa Maria currently lives in Albuquerque. She has lived all over Northern New Mexico, and has spent a lifetime as an artist, photographer and writer. Her work has appeared in numerous anthologies, and her book of poetry, *Lichen Kisses,* was published in 2013.

Reza Saberi is an Iranian translator who worked with Robin Macgowan on the "Saeb & the Ghazal" text in this issue.

Elaine Schwartz resides in Albuquerque, NM where she writes, gardens and works hard to keep up with her two rambunctious grandsons. Her poetry, best described as a tapestry of place and political imagination, has appeared in numerous publications including the *Santa Fe Literary Review, Harwood Anthology, Malpais Review, Blue Collar Review* and *Poetica.*

Jasmine Sena y Cuffee is a native of Albuquerque's South Valley. She leads writing workshops and performs her poetry throughout New Mexico and the Western U.S. She is currently working on her first manuscript of poetry *Where the Arroyos and Train Tracks Meet* and is a contributing artist in many anthologies such as *A Bigger Boat Anthology, Earthships: A New Mecca Poetry Anthology, ¿De Veras? - Voices from the National Hispanic Cultural Center, Malpais Review,* and the ArtStreet Common Threads Synergy Project.

Marilyn Stablein's book of poems *Splitting Hard Ground* won the New Mexico Book Award and the National Federation of Press Women's Book Award. Other books include a series of prose poems based on dreams, *Night Travels to Tibet,* a Himalayan memoir *Sleeping in Caves,* and a collection of eco-essays *Climate of Extremes: Landscape and Imagination.* Book Arts Editions recently published her chapbook, *A Pot of Soup.* Other recent work was published or is forthcoming in *Kyoto Journal, Otoliths, Section8magazine, Gargoyle* and *Fixed & Free Anthology II.* Her art

271

appears on the covers of *Rattle Magazine, Gargoyle, Malpais Review,* and *Raven Chronicles.* Her award-winning artist books are featured in *LARK's 1,000 Artist Books* and *500 Artist Books.* A current exhibition of her artist books is on display at Concordia University's George R. White Library, Portland, Oregon through December. In January she will teach *The Art of Memoir: Your Story Your Way* through the Mountain Writers Series in Portland. She and her husband Gary own Anthology Booksellers in Portland and online. Visit marilynstablein.com.

Judith Toler has been an editor, waitress, keypunch operator, counter of cows, English professor, political activist, faculty union organizer, visual artist and award-winning poet. She began writing poetry fifteen years ago after retiring to Santa Fe, New Mexico from Rochester, New York. Since then, dozens of her poems have appeared in a variety of local and international anthologies and literary magazines. Judith recently published a limited-edition chapbook, *Picasso's Horse,* and is currently organizing her extensive body of work into two books: *My Grandmother's Name Was Grace* and *In the Shine of Broken Things.*

Lawrence Welsh's eighth book of poetry, *Begging for Vultures: New and Selected Poems, 1994-2009,* was published by the University of New Mexico Press. Now in a second printing, this collection won the New Mexico-Arizona Book Award. It was also named a Notable Book by Southwest Books of the Year and a finalist for both the PEN Southwest Book Award and the Writers' League of Texas Book Award. A first generation Irish American and award-winning journalist, Welsh's work has appeared in more than 200 publications.

Cynthia West is known for painting, photography, digital imaging, and book arts. Her works are in collections world-wide. She is the author of five collections of poetry: *For Beauty Way,* 1990, and *1000 Stone Buddhas,* 1993, published by Inked Wingbeat, Santa Fe; *Rainbringer,* 2004, *The New Sun,* 2007 and *In the Center of the Field,* 2010, published by Sunstone Press, Santa Fe. She is currently gathering poems for the next volume. Visit her web site: www.westvision.us.

Holly Wilson began writing poetry as a teen and was involved in poetry readings in the 1970s in Albuquerque and Santa Fe. She studied linguistics at the University of New Mexico and after graduation taught for 13 years in San Diego. She enjoys reconnecting with the vibrant poetry community in New Mexico now that she is back.

Keith Wilson is the featured poet in this issue.

Tanaya Winder is a poet, writer, artist, and educator from the Southern Ute, Duckwater Shoshone, and Pyramid Lake Paiute Nations. A winner of the 2010 A Room of Her Own Foundation's Orlando prize in poetry, her work has appeared or is forthcoming in *Cutthroat* magazine, *Adobe Walls, Superstition Review, Drunkenboat* and *Kweli,* among others. She is a co-founder and editor-in-chief of *As/Us: A Space for Women of the World.*

CREDITS

POEMS

Hakim Bellamy's "A.A. (Afro Anonymous) aka 'In Recovery' aka WARdrobe" © Hakim Bellamy August 15, 2014.

Jane Lipman's "Ballad of an Alpha Male's Daughter" was first published in *White Crow's Secret Life*, Pudding House Publications, 2009; "Borders/Fronteras" was first published in *On the Back Porch of the Moon*, Black Swan Editions, 2012; "Mystery School" was first published in *On the Back Porch of the Moon*, Black Swan Editions, 2012, and in the anthology *Pushing the Envelope: Epistolary Poems*, Jonas Zdanys, editor, 2014.

Mary Oishi's "Women When We Rise" was previously published in *Spirit Birds They Told Me*, West End Press, 2011.

Margaret Randall's "I Do Not Bow My Head" and "Without Warning" are from *About Little Charlie Lindberg*; "La Llorona" is from *The Rhizome as a Field of Broken Bones.*

Georgia Santa Maria's "Letter From My Great-Grandmothers to the Macho-Boys of Politics" was published in *Lichen Kisses*, 2013; "The Vegan Feminist Dilemma" was published in *Adobe Walls*, #5, 2014.

Elaine Schwartz's "Ars Poetica: the writing group" was previously published in *Blue Moon Review*, 2002, Santa Cruz, CA; "Gaza" was previously published on the *Gazal Page*, 2010, and *The Rag*, 2010; "Letter to my sister on the southern shore" was previously published in the *New Mexico State Poetry Society Anthology*, 2013.

Cynthia West's "To My Daughter" appeared in *In the Center of the Field*, Sunstone Press, 2010.

Selections from Saeb's *The Garden of Amazement* have appeared in *Eras* and *The Massachusetts Review*, and in accordion format in a booklet of the same title issued by www.LonghousePoetry.com.

Many thanks to Heloise Wilson for the use of **Keith Wilson's** poems and photo.

Omitted from our Summer 2014 issue: **Michael C Ford's** "TOME #3 Freeze Frame for Edward Dorn" is from *T.O.M.E.S. {Transistorized Oscillator Modulator Envelopes}*; written Boise, 1974.

ART AND PHOTOS

Denise Weaver Ross's images on the cover and the back cover are © Denise Weaver Ross, 2012.

Larry Goodell photo by Lenore Goodell.

Nancy Morejón photo from online at www.ahs.cu.

SUBMISSION GUIDELINES

Malpaís Review is a 6"x9" hardcopy publication between 120 and 220 pages each issue. Reading Periods: for Spring issue: Oct, Nov, Dec; for Summer issue: Jan, Feb, Mar; for Autumn issue: Apr, May, Jun; for Winter issue: Jul, Aug, Sep.

Poems: *Malpaís* Review seeks original poems, previously unpublished in North America, written in English. Any topic, but please no hate-inciting or pornographic work. Submit 1 to 5 poems, no limit on length, but once you hit 10 pages call the submission done (unless the submission is a single poem that is longer than 10 pages). One submission per reading period. Notification of acceptance will take place within 1 month of the closing of a reading period. If your work is accepted into an issue, please let one issue go by before you submit again. In other words, we will publish your work a maximum of twice a year in an effort to keep the voices fresh. No simultaneous submissions. The editor reserves the right to edit and cannot be held liable for the occasional typo or formatting error.

Essay: Topics: poetic criticism, history, theory, a specific poet or poem. Essays should be original and previously unpublished in North America. Length may be up to 5,000 words.

Translations: Translations of both poems and essays will be considered. Required: permission of the original poet is required along with a copy of the poem in its original language (assumes poet is living and/or copyrights are still in force). We intend to publish both the original poem and the translation if space permits.

Featured Poets: Will be invited by the editorial staff for each issue.

Artwork: 1 to 3 digital images should be saved as JPG (JPEG), at a resolution of 300 dpi. Make sure you set your email to attach the "actual" image instead of allowing the email program to reduce the image size. Set images to CYMK. If the image is selected for showing in the interior of the issue, it will be converted to grayscale.

How/Where: Electronic submissions are preferred. Please send your poems in the body of an email. Due to the risk of viruses, we will discard, without reading, all emails with attachments. If your poems have unusual formatting, note it, and we will ask for a file attachment (such as pdf or doc file) if the work is accepted.

In the subject line of the email, please place the words POETRY or ESSAY, a dash, then your name. Example: poetry–JQ Public.

Email ONLY to poetry@Malpaísreview.com.

Please include a short, third-person **biography** with your submission. If you do not have access to email, please send hardcopy to: *Malpaís Review*, po box 339, Placitas, NM 87043. Include a SAS Envelope or Postcard for response. Submissions without SAS Envelope or Postcard will be discarded without reading them.

Submit ARTWORK in a separate email from poems or essays. Artwork may only be submitted via email, to **art@Malpaísreview.com.**

Please include a short, third-person **biography** with your submission.

Rights: *Malpaís* Review seeks first North American Rights of your work to appear in our hardcopy publication, and reserves the right to use your work in a future "best of" issue. Rights revert to author upon publication.

Made in the USA
Monee, IL
17 March 2021

63044334R00151